S0-AWQ-967

Editorial Development: Marilyn Evans
Robyn Raymer
Sarita Chávez Silverman
Susan Rose Simms
Stephanie Wright
Copy Editing: Laurie Westrich
Art Direction: Cheryl Puckett
Cover Design: David Price
Design/Production: Susan Bigger
John D. Williams

EMC 2794

Evan-Moor®
Helping Children Learn

Visit
teaching-standards.com
to view a correlation
of this book.
This is a free service.

**Correlated to
Current Standards**

Weekly Walk-Through

Each week of **A Word a Day** follows the same format, making it easy for both students and teacher to use.

Words of the Week

Four new words are presented each week. A definition, example sentence, and discussion prompts are provided for each word.

Part of Speech The part of speech is identified. You may or may not want to share this information with the class, depending on the skill level of your students.

Definition Each word is defined in a complete sentence. The same definition is found in the reproducible student dictionary, which begins on page 148.

Graphic Organizer Prompt One word each week requires completion of a graphic organizer.

Example Sentence Each new word is used in a sentence designed to provide enough context for students to easily grasp its meaning. The same sentence is found in the reproducible student dictionary, which begins on page 148.

Critical Attributes Prompt Discussion questions are provided that require students to identify features that are and are not attributes of the target word. This is one of the most effective ways to help students recognize subtleties of meaning.

Personal Connection Prompt Students are asked to share an opinion, an idea, or a personal experience that demonstrates their understanding of the new word.

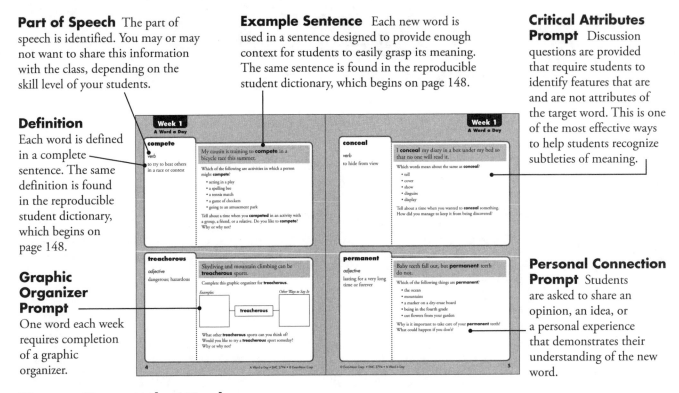

How to Present the Words

Use one of the following methods to present each word:

- Write the word on the board. Then read the definition and the example sentence, explaining as needed before conducting oral activities.

- Make an overhead transparency of the lesson page that shows the word. Then guide students through the definition, example sentence, and oral activities. Make a transparency of page 159 to use with lessons that feature a graphic organizer.

- Reproduce the dictionary on pages 148–158 for each student, or provide each student with a student practice book. (See inside front cover.) Have students find the word in their dictionary, and then guide them through the definition, example sentence, and oral activities.

End-of-Week Review

Review the four words of the week through oral and written activities designed to reinforce student understanding.

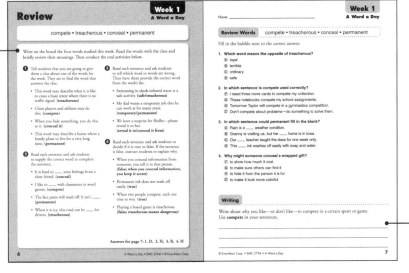

Oral Review
Four oral activities provide you with prompts to review the week's words.

Written Assessment
A student reproducible containing four multiple-choice items and an open-ended writing activity can be used to assess students' mastery.

Additional Features

- Reproducible student dictionary
- Cumulative word index

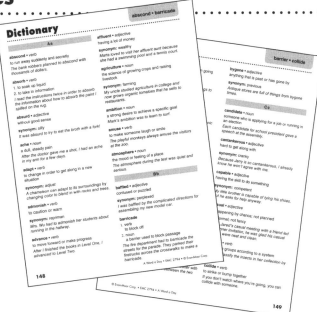

compete

verb

to try to beat others in a race or contest

My cousin is training to **compete** in a bicycle race this summer.

Which of the following are activities in which a person might **compete**?

- acting in a play
- a spelling bee
- a tennis match
- a game of checkers
- going to an amusement park

Tell about a time when you **competed** in an activity with a group, a friend, or a relative. Do you like to **compete**? Why or why not?

treacherous

adjective

dangerous; hazardous

Skydiving and mountain climbing can be **treacherous** sports.

Complete this graphic organizer for **treacherous**.

Examples:

Other Ways to Say It:

treacherous

What other **treacherous** sports can you think of? Would you like to try a **treacherous** sport someday? Why or why not?

A Word a Day • EMC 2794 • © Evan-Moor Corp.

conceal

verb

to hide from view

I **conceal** my diary in a box under my bed so that no one will read it.

Which words mean about the same as **conceal**?

- tell
- cover
- show
- disguise
- display

Tell about a time when you wanted to **conceal** something. How did you manage to keep it from being discovered?

permanent

adjective

lasting for a very long time or forever

Baby teeth fall out, but **permanent** teeth do not.

Which of the following things are **permanent**?

- the ocean
- mountains
- a marker on a dry-erase board
- being in the fourth grade
- cut flowers from your garden

Why is it important to take care of your **permanent** teeth? What could happen if you don't?

Review

compete • treacherous • conceal • permanent

Write on the board the four words studied this week. Read the words with the class and briefly review their meanings. Then conduct the oral activities below.

1 Tell students that you are going to give them a clue about one of the words for the week. They are to find the word that answers the clue.

- This word may describe what it is like to cross a busy street where there is no traffic signal. **(treacherous)**

- Chess players and athletes may do this. **(compete)**

- When you hide something, you do this to it. **(conceal it)**

- This word may describe a home where a family plans to live for a very long time. **(permanent)**

2 Read each sentence and ask students to supply the correct word to complete the sentence.

- It is hard to _____ your feelings from a close friend. **(conceal)**

- I like to _____ with classmates in word games. **(compete)**

- The face paint will wash off. It isn't _____. **(permanent)**

- When it is icy, this road can be _____ for drivers. **(treacherous)**

3 Read each sentence and ask students to tell which word or words are wrong. Then have them provide the correct word from the week's list.

- Swimming in shark-infested water is a safe activity. **(safe/treacherous)**

- My dad wants a temporary job that he can work at for many years. **(temporary/permanent)**

- We have a surprise for Shelby—please reveal it to her. **(reveal it to/conceal it from)**

4 Read each sentence and ask students to decide if it is true or false. If the sentence is false, instruct students to explain why.

- When you conceal information from someone, you tell it to that person. **(false; when you conceal information, you keep it secret)**

- Permanent ink does not wash off easily. **(true)**

- When two people compete, each one tries to win. **(true)**

- Playing a board game is treacherous. **(false; *treacherous* means *dangerous*)**

Answers for page 7: 1. D, 2. H, 3. B, 4. H

Name _____

compete • treacherous • conceal • permanent

Fill in the bubble next to the correct answer.

1. **Which word means the opposite of *treacherous*?**
   Ⓐ loyal
   Ⓑ terrible
   Ⓒ ordinary
   Ⓓ safe

2. **In which sentence is *compete* used correctly?**
   Ⓕ I need three more cards to compete my collection.
   Ⓖ These notebooks compete my school assignments.
   Ⓗ Tomorrow Taylor will compete in a gymnastics competition.
   Ⓙ Don't compete about problems—do something to solve them.

3. **In which sentence could *permanent* fill in the blank?**
   Ⓐ Rain is a ____ weather condition.
   Ⓑ Granny is visiting us, but her ____ home is in Iowa.
   Ⓒ Our ____ teacher taught the class for one week only.
   Ⓓ This ____ ink washes off easily with soap and water.

4. **Why might someone *conceal* a wrapped gift?**
   Ⓕ to show how much it cost
   Ⓖ to make sure others can find it
   Ⓗ to hide it from the person it is for
   Ⓙ to make it look more colorful

Writing

Write about why you like—or don't like—to compete in a certain sport or game.
Use **compete** in your sentences.

_____

_____

_____

precious

adjective

1. rare and valuable
2. special or dear

My most **precious** possession is this ring with four **precious** gems in the setting.

Complete this graphic organizer for **precious**.

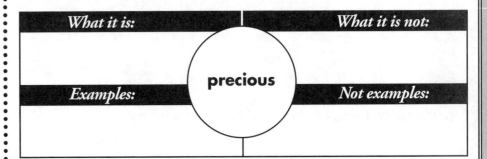

What it is:	*What it is not:*
	precious	
Examples:	*Not examples:*

Tell about something that is very **precious** to you. Is it **precious** because it is worth a lot of money or because it is dear to you?

---

sluggish

adjective

moving slowly; lacking energy

After eating a big lunch and resting in the hammock, I felt so **sluggish** that I could barely move.

Which words mean about the same as **sluggish**?

- energetic
- tired
- slow
- lively
- sleepy

Tell about a time when you felt **sluggish**. Why did you feel this way, and what did you do to get your energy back? What kinds of things make you feel **sluggish**?

discussion

noun

a talk about things

synonym:
conversation

Our teacher gathered us in a circle for a **discussion** about our upcoming field trip.

Which of the following might you do in a **discussion**?

- take a nap
- listen to other people
- offer your opinion
- ask questions
- brush your teeth

Tell about a time when you had a **discussion** in class or with friends. What was it about?

How does a **discussion** help people share their ideas?

advance

verb

to move forward or make progress

After I finished the books in Level One, I **advanced** to Level Two.

On a game board, which commands would help a player **advance**?

- "Lose your turn."
- "Move forward to GO."
- "Take another turn!"
- "Move back 3 spaces."
- "Skip ahead 2 spaces."

Tell about a time when you were working on something and got to **advance** to the next level.

Why is it important to finish one thing before you **advance** to the next?

Review

precious • sluggish • discussion • advance

Write on the board the four words studied this week. Read the words with the class and briefly review their meanings. Then conduct the oral activities below.

1 Tell students that you are going to give them a clue about one of the words for the week. They are to find the word that answers the clue.

- Two friends might have one on the phone. (**a discussion**)

- Students do this when they finish one grade and start another. (**advance**)

- This word describes your most prized possession. (**precious**)

- You would probably feel this way if you hadn't gotten enough sleep. (**sluggish**)

2 Read each sentence and ask students to supply the correct word to complete the sentence.

- When I ____ to the next level, the video game will become more challenging. (**advance**)

- I felt ____ after eating a huge Thanksgiving dinner. (**sluggish**)

- Grandma made me this quilt, so it's very ____ to me. (**precious**)

- After reading the book, our class had a ____ about it. (**discussion**)

3 Read each sentence and ask students to tell which word is wrong. Then have them provide the correct word from the week's list.

- Oh no! I've lost my worthless gold necklace! (**worthless/precious**)

- When an army moves forward, it retreats. (**retreats/advances**)

- After flying on an airplane for twelve hours, I felt energetic. (**energetic/sluggish**)

4 Read each sentence and ask students to decide if it is true or false. If the sentence is false, instruct students to explain why.

- To have a discussion, you need at least two people. (**true**)

- Something that is precious to you may not be precious to others. (**true**)

- Feeling sluggish makes it easier to play sports. (**false; you move slowly when you feel sluggish**)

- The word *advance* means the opposite of *retreat*. (**true**)

Answers for page 11: 1. C, 2. G, 3. A, 4. H

Review Words precious • sluggish • discussion • advance

Fill in the bubble next to the correct answer.

1. **Which word means the opposite of *sluggish*?**
   - Ⓐ kind
   - Ⓑ intelligent
   - Ⓒ energetic
   - Ⓓ beautiful

2. **In which sentence is *discussion* used correctly?**
   - Ⓕ We took our discussion along on a trip to the beach.
   - Ⓖ We had a wonderful discussion on books and movies.
   - Ⓗ Natalie competed in a gymnastics discussion last week.
   - Ⓙ Dad plans to plant a discussion in our garden next spring.

3. **In which sentence could *precious* fill in the blank?**
   - Ⓐ After a long dry spell, rain seems very ____.
   - Ⓑ I saw a big, ____ spider on the ceiling over my bed.
   - Ⓒ Please keep your rude, ____ comments to yourself!
   - Ⓓ Every day Mom makes me a ____ sandwich for lunch.

4. **What happens when an army *advances*?**
   - Ⓕ It turns around.
   - Ⓖ It surrenders to its enemy.
   - Ⓗ It moves forward.
   - Ⓙ It loses a big battle.

Writing

Write about a dream or goal that is precious to you. Use **precious** in your sentences.

_____

_____

_____

boost

noun

something that
lifts you up,
either physically
or emotionally

I couldn't reach the doorbell, so my brother gave me a **boost**.

In which of these situations might you need a **boost**?

- when you're feeling sad
- when you're trying to climb a tall tree
- when you're digging in the sand
- when you can't reach the top shelf
- when you're happy and excited

Tell about a time when someone did or said something that gave you a **boost**. Have you ever given someone else a **boost**? How did it feel?

barrier

noun

something that
prevents things from
going through

synonym: obstruction

The people made a **barrier** of sandbags to keep the river from flooding their town.

Which of the following could be a **barrier**?

- a brick wall
- an iron gate
- an open field
- a locked door
- the sky

Why are **barriers** set up to block off streets during a parade? In what other situations are **barriers** used?

recommend

verb

to praise the value of something; suggest as worthwhile

synonym: endorse

I **recommend** you try the milkshakes at the local diner; they're delicious!

Which of these statements would you use to **recommend** a product?

- "That shampoo got my hair really clean!"
- "This cereal gets soggy so quickly."
- "That movie was so boring it put me to sleep."
- "This game is too complicated."
- "These shoes will help you run fast!"

Tell about a time when someone **recommended** a book or movie to you. Did you read or see it? What is a book or movie that you have **recommended** to others?

gratitude

noun

a feeling of being grateful and thankful

When Dad gave me a new computer game, I showed my **gratitude** by giving him a big hug.

Complete this graphic organizer for **gratitude**.

Examples: *Other Ways to Say It:*

gratitude

Tell about a time when you showed **gratitude** for something someone did for you. Tell about a time when someone showed **gratitude** to you for something you did.

boost • barrier • recommend • gratitude

Write on the board the four words studied this week. Read the words with the class and briefly review their meanings. Then conduct the oral activities below.

1 Tell students that you are going to give them a clue about one of the words for the week. They are to find the word that answers the clue.

- A dam is one. **(a barrier)**

- If you enjoyed reading a certain book, you might do this.
  (recommend it to others)

- You might need one in order to get up on a horse. **(a boost)**

- This is a feeling of thankfulness.
  (gratitude)

2 Read each sentence and ask students to supply the correct word to complete the sentence.

- I _____ the yummy apple pie at Marie's Restaurant. **(recommend)**

- I felt sad, but my dog gave me a _____ by licking my hand. **(boost)**

- Saying "thank you" is a simple way to show _____. **(gratitude)**

- This tall fence provides a _____ between the construction site and the sidewalk.
  (barrier)

3 Read each sentence and ask students to tell which word or words are wrong. Then have them provide the correct word from the week's list.

- I oppose using Hairific Shampoo—it smells great and leaves hair squeaky clean. **(oppose/recommend)**

- To keep our dog and cats apart, we set up an opening between them.
  (an opening/a barrier)

- When his family gave him a surprise birthday party, Alex was filled with ungratefulness.
  (ungratefulness/gratitude)

4 Read each sentence and ask students to decide if it is true or false. If the sentence is false, instruct students to explain why.

- For a sick person, a get-well card can be a boost. **(true)**

- People don't normally recommend books that they have not read. **(true)**

- You could show gratitude by frowning at someone. **(false; if you felt thankful, you would probably smile, not frown)**

- A stone wall is a barrier. **(true)**

Answers for page 15: 1. D, 2. J, 3. B, 4. G

Review Words   boost • barrier • recommend • gratitude

Fill in the bubble next to the correct answer.

1. Which word means the opposite of *barrier*?

Ⓐ roof

Ⓑ wall

Ⓒ fence

Ⓓ opening

2. In which sentence is *boost* used correctly?

Ⓕ I have a boost: let's do our homework at my house.

Ⓖ For dinner last night, we had potatoes and baked boost.

Ⓗ I threw the boost and one of my teammates caught it.

Ⓙ A bouquet of flowers may give a sick person a boost.

3. In which sentence could *recommend* fill in the blank?

Ⓐ We ____ our dog each afternoon at about 5:00.

Ⓑ I asked the waitress to ____ something on the menu.

Ⓒ Mom and Dad ____ their car at Fresco's Car Wash.

Ⓓ Will you ____ this math problem? I don't understand it.

4. When would you be most likely to feel *gratitude*?

Ⓕ when you're having a bad day

Ⓖ when someone does you a favor

Ⓗ while you're brushing your teeth

Ⓙ while you're doing your homework

Writing

Write about a band or singer whose music you would recommend to other kids.
Use **recommend** in your sentences.

_____

_____

_____

participant

noun

someone who joins in an activity

The winner of the race will receive a medal, but all **participants** will receive a T-shirt.

Which of these is a **participant**?

- a member of a volleyball team
- a person watching a soccer game
- someone who enters a coloring contest
- someone who rides in a car
- a member of the cast of the school play

Tell about a time when you were a **participant** in an activity. Then think of a time when you were not a **participant**, but watched others. Which do you think is more fun?

temporary

adjective

something that lasts only for a short time

The power outage was **temporary**; our electricity was back on by morning.

Which of the following mean about the same as **temporary**?

- momentary
- forever
- changing
- long-lasting
- passing

What was a **temporary** problem you had? How long did it last?

purchase

verb

to buy something

Our family tries to **purchase** things when they're on sale.

Which of the following can you use to **purchase** something?

- a check
- money
- chewing gum
- a credit card
- trading cards

Tell about a time when you **purchased** something with money you earned. How did it feel to **purchase** something with your own money?

ignore

verb

to pay no attention to something

If someone teases you, just **ignore** him or her and walk away.

Complete the graphic organizer for **ignore**.

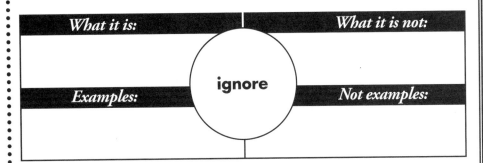

Tell about a time when you **ignored** someone or something because that was the right thing to do. Now tell about a time when you **ignored** someone or something and it was not the right thing to do.

participant • temporary • purchase • ignore

Write on the board the four words studied this week. Read the words with the class and briefly review their meanings. Then conduct the oral activities below.

1 Tell students that you are going to give them a clue about one of the words for the week. They are to find the word that answers the clue.

- If someone tries to bother you, you should do this. (**ignore that person**)

- Shoppers do this. (**purchase things**)

- This word can be used to describe a situation that isn't permanent. (**temporary**)

- If you enter a contest or join in a group activity, you are one of these. (**a participant**)

2 Read each sentence and ask students to supply the correct word to complete the sentence.

- Please don't ____ your little brother— he needs your attention. (**ignore**)

- Here is a ____ library card. Your permanent one will come in the mail next month. (**temporary**)

- Each contest ____ will receive a free T-shirt. (**participant**)

- We need to ____ bread and milk at the grocery store. (**purchase**)

3 Read each sentence and ask students to tell which word or words are wrong. Then have them provide the correct word from the week's list.

- I'm saving my money to sell a new bicycle. (**sell/purchase**)

- Try to focus on silly details that don't matter. (**focus on/ignore**)

- After the flood, the city provided permanent housing in tents to those whose homes were damaged. (**permanent/temporary**)

4 Read each sentence and ask students to decide if it is true or false. If the sentence is false, instruct students to explain why.

- If you join in an activity, you are a participant. (**true**)

- It is rude to ignore a friend who says hi to you. (**true**)

- People go to a library to purchase books. (**false; you don't buy books at a library, you borrow them**)

- If you live in a town all of your life, that town is your temporary home. (**false; that town is your permanent home**)

Answers for page 19: 1. C, 2. F, 3. B, 4. H

Review Words   participant • temporary • purchase • ignore

Fill in the bubble next to the correct answer.

1. **Which word means the opposite of *temporary*?**
   - Ⓐ difficult
   - Ⓑ unusual
   - Ⓒ permanent
   - Ⓓ boring

2. **In which sentence is *purchase* used correctly?**
   - Ⓕ Mom took me to the store to purchase some new shoes.
   - Ⓖ I took my dog to the park so she could purchase her ball.
   - Ⓗ During discussions, we purchase ideas with classmates.
   - Ⓙ I purchase my clothes every morning before breakfast.

3. **In which sentence could *participant* fill in the blank?**
   - Ⓐ Grandpa Maxwell is our oldest family ____.
   - Ⓑ I hope to be a ____ in next year's writing contest.
   - Ⓒ I've known Shelby since I was four—she's my best ____.
   - Ⓓ A ____ came to our front door and delivered a package.

4. **Which of these people should you try to *ignore*?**
   - Ⓕ your school principal, who is making an announcement
   - Ⓖ your grandparent, who is telling funny family stories
   - Ⓗ a fifth-grader who is spreading mean stories about others
   - Ⓙ a librarian who is explaining how to find the book you need

Writing

Write about a time when you purchased something and later wished you hadn't bought that item. Use **purchase** in your sentences.

_____

_____

_____

decline

verb

to turn down or refuse something

Mike had to **decline** the invitation to his friend's party because his family was going to be out of town.

Which statements might you make to **decline** something?

- "Thank you, but I'm too full for dessert."
- "I'm sorry, but I won't be able to go."
- "Thank you for that nice invitation."
- "I would love to come over today!"
- "I'm afraid I just can't do that."

Tell about a time when you had to **decline** an invitation. What is a polite way to **decline** an invitation or a request?

plunge

verb

1. to dive into water
2. to fall sharply

Standing at the edge of the boat, my heart **plunged** as I watched my necklace **plunge** into the sea.

Which of these demonstrate a meaning of **plunge**?

- The temperature dropped 30 degrees in one hour.
- A kite rose on the wind.
- Put your hand into the full sink and pull the stopper.
- The Labrador leaped off the dock to retrieve the stick.
- The price of a gallon of gasoline is half of what it was last week.

When would you want to **plunge** into a swimming pool? When wouldn't you want to **plunge** into a swimming pool? For what item would you like to see the price **plunge**?

capable

adjective

having the skill to do something

synonym: competent

My little brother is **capable** of tying his shoes, but he asks for help anyway.

Which of the following might you be **capable** of doing?

- lifting a car
- brushing your hair
- pouring a bowl of cereal
- spelling all the words in the dictionary
- making your bed

What is something you are **capable** of doing? What is something you want to become **capable** of doing in the future?

massive

adjective

extraordinarily large, heavy, and solid

It took eight men to move the **massive** oak table into the moving van.

Complete the graphic organizer for **massive**.

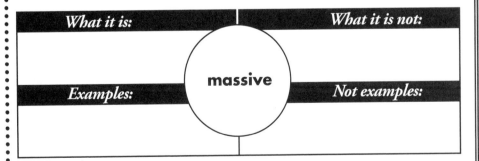

What is the most **massive** thing you have in your home? About how many people would it take to lift it?

decline • plunge • capable • massive

Write on the board the four words studied this week. Read the words with the class and briefly review their meanings. Then conduct the oral activities below.

1 Tell students that you are going to give them a clue about one of the words for the week. They are to find the word that answers the clue.

- You could use this word to describe a whale. **(massive)**

- You might do this at the lake if it were 105° outside. **(plunge into the lake)**

- You do this if someone invites you to a party that you can't go to. **(decline the invitation)**

- You could use this word to describe a man who is able to lift a car. **(capable)**

2 Read each sentence and ask students to supply the correct word to complete the sentence.

- I'm not ____ of lifting my dad. **(capable)**

- A landslide occurs when rocks ____ down the side of a mountain. **(plunge)**

- I have to work that day, so I must ____ your offer of movie tickets. **(decline)**

- A ____ mudslide blocked the highway. **(massive)**

3 Read each sentence and ask students to tell which word is wrong. Then have them provide the correct word from the week's list.

- I have other plans on Saturday, so I'll have to accept your invitation. **(accept/decline)**

- A tiny elephant stomped through the jungle. **(tiny/massive)**

- At the party there was a contest to find coins in the pool, so all the kids waded right in. **(waded/plunged)**

4 Read each sentence and ask students to decide if it is true or false. If the sentence is false, instruct students to explain why.

- An adult bison, or buffalo, is massive. **(true)**

- Most three-year-olds are capable of speaking. **(true)**

- People who drive big cars wish that the price of gasoline would plunge. **(true)**

- If you can't go to a party, you must decline the invitation. **(true)**

Answers for page 23: 1. A, 2. J, 3. B, 4. G

Name _____

Review Words   decline • plunge • capable • massive

Fill in the bubble next to the correct answer.

1. **Which word means the opposite of *massive*?**
   Ⓐ tiny
   Ⓑ huge
   Ⓒ fierce
   Ⓓ gentle

2. **Which word means the opposite of *decline*?**
   Ⓕ refuse
   Ⓖ sell
   Ⓗ purchase
   Ⓙ accept

3. **In which sentence could *plunge* fill in the blank?**
   Ⓐ Slowly and sadly, they ____ down the street.
   Ⓑ You'll cool off if you ____ into the pool.
   Ⓒ The mountains look like they ____ up to the sky.
   Ⓓ Snails ____ along the sidewalk in the early mornings.

4. **A five-year-old child is *capable* of which activity?**
   Ⓕ piloting a space shuttle
   Ⓖ tying his or her shoes
   Ⓗ lifting a 200-pound weight
   Ⓙ reading a college textbook

Writing

Write about a massive creature. Use **massive** in your sentences.

_____

_____

_____

thaw

verb

to melt after
being frozen

The frozen turkey must **thaw** in the
refrigerator for three days before we can cook it.

Which of the following could **thaw**?

- icy streets
- a light bulb
- warm laundry
- a frozen pond or lake
- peas taken out of the freezer

What causes a frozen pond to **thaw**? What can you do to
make frozen food **thaw** more quickly?

symphony

noun

a long piece of music
played by an orchestra

The famous composer Mozart wrote a
symphony that was nicknamed "Jupiter."

Which sounds would you probably hear in a **symphony**?

- a cello
- a piano
- banging pots and pans
- a coach's whistle
- a drum

Have you ever listened to a **symphony**? How does the music
make you feel? If you could perform a **symphony**, which
instrument in the orchestra would you like to play?

spontaneous

adjective

happening without planning

I wasn't expecting the joke to be funny, but I let out a **spontaneous** laugh.

Which of the following are examples of **spontaneous** actions?

- A team of climbers scales Mt. Everest.
- A family decides at 6:30 to see the 7:00 movie at the theater.
- You reserve the skating rink for your birthday party.
- You and your friend decide to switch shoes at recess.
- Your family starts planning a vacation a year ahead.

Do you think a **spontaneous** activity can be more fun than a planned one? Why? What's the advantage of planning ahead of time? What's the advantage of being **spontaneous**?

rickety

adjective

likely to fall over or fall apart due to weakness

The **rickety** old fence blew over with the first strong winter wind.

Complete the graphic organizer for **rickety**.

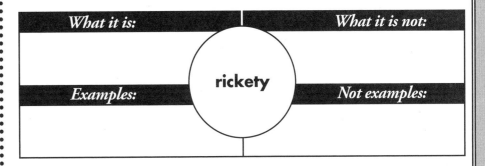

What it is:		*What it is not:*
	rickety	
Examples:		*Not examples:*

Why is it a good idea to be careful with something that is **rickety**? Why shouldn't you use something that's **rickety** until it's fixed?

Review

thaw • symphony • spontaneous • rickety

Write on the board the four words studied this week. Read the words with the class and briefly review their meanings. Then conduct the oral activities below.

1 Tell students that you are going to give them a clue about one of the words for the week. They are to find the word that answers the clue.

- You could use this word to describe an old staircase that is falling apart. **(rickety)**

- An orchestra plays this type of musical piece. **(a symphony)**

- You could use this word to describe an unplanned party. **(spontaneous)**

- Frozen ponds do this when the weather warms in the springtime. **(thaw)**

2 Read each sentence and ask students to supply the correct word to complete the sentence.

- The orchestra played a ____ by Beethoven, a famous composer. **(symphony)**

- Don't drive your car over that ____ old bridge! **(rickety)**

- Let's go ice-skating before the frozen pond begins to ____. **(thaw)**

- The sun came out today, so we had a ____ picnic in the backyard. **(spontaneous)**

3 Read each sentence and ask students to tell which word or words are wrong. Then have them provide the correct word from the week's list.

- Take the chicken out of the freezer so that it will harden in time for dinner. **(harden/thaw)**

- That strong, steady ladder is very dangerous to climb. **(strong, steady/rickety)**

- This planned event happened on the spur of the moment. **(planned/spontaneous)**

- The large orchestra played a little tune that went on for an hour. **(little tune/symphony)**

4 Read each sentence and ask students to decide if it is true or false. If the sentence is false, instruct students to explain why.

- Symphonies are dances. **(false; they are orchestral pieces)**

- A rickety ladder is unsafe. **(true)**

- People make detailed plans for spontaneous events. **(false; such events happen without planning)**

- Frozen ponds usually thaw when winter begins. **(false; they usually thaw in springtime)**

Answers for page 27: 1. C, 2. J, 3. B, 4. G

Name _____

Fill in the bubble next to the correct answer.

1. **Which word means the opposite of *rickety*?**
   Ⓐ narrow
   Ⓑ huge
   Ⓒ steady
   Ⓓ smooth

2. **Which word means the opposite of *thaw*?**
   Ⓕ separate
   Ⓖ combine
   Ⓗ melt
   Ⓙ freeze

3. **In which sentence could *spontaneous* fill in the blank?**
   Ⓐ We made our ＿＿ vacation plans about six months ago.
   Ⓑ We had a ＿＿ party when some friends came by unexpectedly.
   Ⓒ It took many weeks of planning to set up this ＿＿ dinner party.
   Ⓓ Each year at this time our school has a ＿＿ fair to raise money.

4. **Who performs a *symphony*?**
   Ⓕ famous movie actors
   Ⓖ orchestra musicians
   Ⓗ magicians
   Ⓙ gymnasts

Writing

Write about a spontaneous event that you enjoyed. Use **spontaneous** in your sentences.

_____

_____

_____

resource

noun

a person or thing that is a source of help or support

The library is a great **resource** for learning about American history.

Which of the following are examples of **resources**?

- a dictionary
- a teacher
- a Scout leader
- an encyclopedia
- a grocery store receipt

What kind of **resources** have you used to find information for your schoolwork? Which people can be a **resource** for you? In what ways?

predicament

noun

a difficult, dangerous, or unpleasant situation

The sailors were in a **predicament** when the mainsail ripped.

Which of these mean about the same as **predicament**?

- a fix
- a jam
- a parade
- a mess
- a contest

Tell about a time when you found yourself in a **predicament**. How did you get out of it?

perplexed

adjective

confused; uncertain

I was **perplexed** because the directions to the museum did not make sense to me.

Which words mean about the same as **perplexed**?

- sure
- certain
- puzzled
- confused
- unsure

How have you figured out something that you were **perplexed** about? What are some good strategies for understanding something **perplexing**?

unruly

adjective

hard to control; wild

The **unruly** crowd went wild when the rock stars appeared.

Complete the graphic organizer for **unruly**.

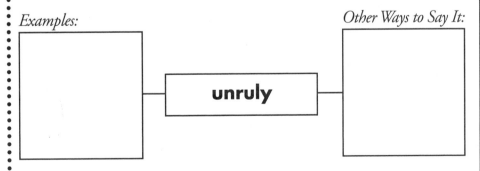

Examples: *Other Ways to Say It:*

unruly

Have you ever seen someone act **unruly**? How did it make you feel? Is it ever all right to be **unruly**? When?

Review

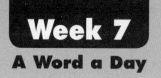

---

resource • predicament • perplexed • unruly

Write on the board the four words studied this week. Read the words with the class and briefly review their meanings. Then conduct the oral activities below.

1 Tell students that you are going to give them a clue about one of the words for the week. They are to find the word that answers the clue.

- You could use this word to describe 20 toddlers at a birthday party. **(unruly)**

- A difficult math problem might make you feel this way. **(perplexed)**

- A dictionary is one. **(a resource)**

- If you were in one of these, you would probably try to get out of it. **(a predicament)**

2 Read each sentence and ask students to supply the correct word to complete the sentence.

- Our dog was very _____ until we took her to obedience training. **(unruly)**

- When I want to learn more about the mid-1900s, I use my grandma as a _____. **(resource)**

- How can I manage to get myself out of this _____? **(predicament)**

- Zack looks _____. Please explain the situation to him. **(perplexed)**

3 Read each sentence and ask students to tell which word or words are wrong. Then have them provide the correct word from the week's list.

- This opportunity is one of the worst messes I've ever been in. **(opportunity/predicament)**

- You look so sure that I can tell you don't understand what I said. **(sure/perplexed)**

- How can one trainer handle five calm, obedient dogs at once? **(calm, obedient/unruly)**

- When I need advice about a personal matter, my Aunt Julia is no help at all. **(no help at all/a resource)**

4 Read each sentence and ask students to decide if it is true or false. If the sentence is false, instruct students to explain why.

- An encyclopedia is a resource, and so is a science book. **(true)**

- You would be in a predicament if you forgot to study for an important test. **(true)**

- Puppies can be unruly. **(true)**

- When you are perplexed about something, you understand it. **(false; you don't understand it)**

Answers for page 31: 1. A, 2. H, 3. B, 4. J

Name _____

Fill in the bubble next to the correct answer.

1. **Which word means the opposite of *unruly*?**
   - Ⓐ obedient
   - Ⓑ clever
   - Ⓒ stylish
   - Ⓓ educated

2. **Which word has the same meaning as *perplexed*?**
   - Ⓕ hungry
   - Ⓖ thirsty
   - Ⓗ confused
   - Ⓙ exhausted

3. **In which sentence could *predicament* fill in the blank?**
   - Ⓐ My cousin has a ____ to earn a college scholarship.
   - Ⓑ We must find a way to get ourselves out of this ____.
   - Ⓒ I joined a ____ for students who like math and science.
   - Ⓓ Please join us next Saturday for Katrina's birthday ____.

4. **How can a *resource* help you?**
   - Ⓕ You can eat it if you are hungry.
   - Ⓖ You can sleep on it if you are tired.
   - Ⓗ It can keep you company if you are lonely.
   - Ⓙ It can provide facts that you want to know.

Writing

Write about something that perplexed you when you were younger, but that you now understand. Use **perplexed** in your sentences.

_____

_____

_____

compass

noun

a tool that can help you figure out in which direction you are facing

We knew that the camp was to the southwest, so we used our **compass** to help us find our way back to it.

Which directions would be on a **compass**?

- west
- south
- forward
- northeast
- sideways

In what situations would it be a good idea to have a **compass** with you?

atmosphere

noun

the mood or feeling of a place

The **atmosphere** during the test was quiet and serious.

What kind of **atmosphere** would you expect to find at:

- a birthday party?
- the library?
- a football game?
- the circus?
- a hospital?

Describe the **atmosphere** in your classroom right now. How is the **atmosphere** on the playground different from that in the library or your classroom?

collide

verb

to strike or
bump together

If you don't watch where you're going, you can **collide** with someone.

Which of these are things that might **collide**?

- flowers in the garden
- mountain bikers on a trail
- cars at an intersection
- swimmers with their eyes closed
- books on a shelf

What might happen when two people **collide**? Have you ever **collided** with someone? What can you say to someone when you accidentally **collide** with him or her?

criticize

verb

to tell someone about
what he or she
has done wrong

Father **criticized** the young child's poor table manners.

Complete the graphic organizer for **criticize**.

Examples:

criticize

Other Ways to Say It:

Tell about a time when someone **criticized** you. How did you feel? What would be a nice way to **criticize** a person to help him or her make a positive change?

Review

compass • atmosphere • collide • criticize

Write on the board the four words studied this week. Read the words with the class and briefly review their meanings. Then conduct the oral activities below.

1 Tell students that you are going to give them a clue about one of the words for the week. They are to find the word that answers the clue.

- If a classmate says something mean to another student, you might do this. **(criticize him or her)**

- If you don't look where you're going in a crowd, you may do this. **(collide with someone)**

- This is a tool with directions marked on it. **(a compass)**

- This is a synonym for *mood*. **(atmosphere)**

2 Read each sentence and ask students to supply the correct word to complete the sentence.

- The movie was about a meteor that was about to ____ with Planet Earth. **(collide)**

- Please don't ____ me for things that are not my fault. **(criticize)**

- Joe's ____ showed that he was traveling northeast. **(compass)**

- There was a sorrowful ____ in the room after we found out that our pet hamster had died. **(atmosphere)**

3 Read each list of words and phrases. Ask students to supply the word that fits best with each.

- crash into each other, bump into something **(collide)**

- mood, feeling, sad, serious, lighthearted **(atmosphere)**

- travel aid, directions, north, south, east, west **(compass)**

- scold, list faults, object to wrongdoing **(criticize)**

4 Read each sentence and ask students to decide if it is true or false. If the sentence is false, instruct students to explain why.

- When you swing a baseball bat, you hope it will collide with the ball. **(true)**

- Weddings have a joyful atmosphere. **(true)**

- A compass tells how hot or cold the air is. **(false; a compass tells which direction someone is facing)**

- You could criticize someone by yelling "Way to go!" **(false; you criticize people for wrongdoing, not for doing well)**

Answers for page 35: 1. D, 2. H, 3. D, 4. G

| **Review Words** | compass • atmosphere • collide • criticize |

Fill in the bubble next to the correct answer.

1. **Which word means the opposite of *criticize*?**
   Ⓐ instruct
   Ⓑ describe
   Ⓒ avoid
   Ⓓ praise

2. **Which phrase has the same meaning as *collide*?**
   Ⓕ chase after
   Ⓖ jump around
   Ⓗ bump into
   Ⓙ slide past

3. **In which sentence could *atmosphere* fill in the blank?**
   Ⓐ Please turn down the _____ on your CD player.
   Ⓑ We found ourselves in a huge _____ with wooden floors.
   Ⓒ What kind of _____ do you want to be when you grow up?
   Ⓓ The Boyntons' home has a relaxed, happy _____.

4. **How can a *compass* help you?**
   Ⓕ You can drink it if you are thirsty.
   Ⓖ It can help you find your way if you are lost.
   Ⓗ It can keep you company if you are lonely.
   Ⓙ It can tell you words' spellings and definitions.

| **Writing** |

Write about the atmosphere in a place you like to visit. Use **atmosphere** in your sentences.

_____

_____

_____

determined

adjective

showing a firm decision to do something

No matter how tired he got, Harry was **determined** to finish the race.

Which statements would a **determined** person make?

- "I'm definitely going, and that's all there is to it!"
- "I'm not really sure if I want to do that."
- "I'm happy to do whatever you say."
- "Nothing's going to stop me!"
- "I will win that prize."

What is something you are **determined** to do? How can you make sure you are able to do it?

dilemma

noun

a situation that requires a difficult choice

synonym:
predicament

Bonnie's **dilemma** was whether to attend her best friend's birthday party or play in the championship soccer game.

Which of these situations is a **dilemma**?

- You broke your mother's vase and you're afraid to tell her.
- Your friend offers you a choice of one or two chocolates.
- You want to ride your bike, but it's raining.
- You get to choose whether to play in the first or second half of the game.
- Your parents let you choose between a vacation at the beach or in the mountains.

Tell about a time when you faced a **dilemma**. What were the choices you had to make? How did you solve your **dilemma**?

random

adjective

not following any pattern or order

The teacher put everyone's name in a jar and drew the teams in **random** order.

Which of the following could be arranged in **random** order?

- a calendar
- letters in a word
- names in a phone book
- a list of items in your room
- a list of things to buy at the store

What is something you do each day that can be done in **random** order? What is something that must happen in a particular order?

obvious

adjective

very easy to see or understand

It was **obvious** from the smile on her face that she was happy to see her grandmother.

Complete the graphic organizer for **obvious**.

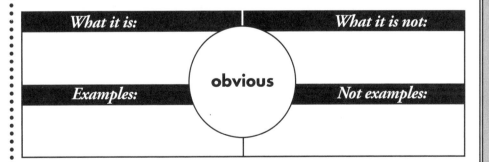

What it is:		*What it is not:*
	obvious	
Examples:		*Not examples:*

What makes it **obvious** that somebody is upset?
What makes it **obvious** that someone is in a good mood?

determined • dilemma • random • obvious

Write on the board the four words studied this week. Read the words with the class and briefly review their meanings. Then conduct the oral activities below.

1 Tell students that you are going to give them a clue about one of the words for the week. They are to find the word that answers the clue.

- This word describes something that is clear to all. **(obvious)**

- You have one when you face a difficult choice. **(a dilemma)**

- Someone who feels this way has made a firm decision to do something. **(determined)**

- If you pick a number this way, you don't follow any pattern or order. **(in random order)**

2 Read each sentence and ask students to supply the correct word to complete the sentence.

- We will choose the winner in _____ order by drawing one slip of paper from a box. **(random)**

- It's _____ that little Anna ate the candy. She has chocolate all over her face. **(obvious)**

- If you are _____ to quit the game, I guess we'll try to finish without you. **(determined)**

- My _____ is whether to vote for Chloe or Sam. **(dilemma)**

3 Read each sentence and ask students to tell which word or words are wrong. Then have them provide the correct word from the week's list.

- I'm wondering whether to go, no matter what! **(wondering whether/determined)**

- Her tears make it unclear that she's sad. **(unclear/obvious)**

- Raffle winners are drawn in alphabetical order. **(alphabetical/random)**

4 Read each sentence and ask students to decide if it is true or false. If the sentence is false, instruct students to explain why.

- It's easy to choose when you have a dilemma. **(false; a dilemma is a hard decision)**

- A determined person does not give up easily. **(true)**

- A random choice does not follow a pattern. **(true)**

- It's always obvious when two boys are twins. **(false; twins do not always look alike)**

Answers for page 39: 1. D, 2. J, 3. C, 4. G

| Review Words | determined • dilemma • random • obvious |

Fill in the bubble next to the correct answer.

1. Which word means the opposite of *obvious*?
- Ⓐ simple
- Ⓑ serious
- Ⓒ silly
- Ⓓ unclear

2. Which word means the opposite of *random*?
- Ⓕ chance
- Ⓖ accidental
- Ⓗ messy
- Ⓙ planned

3. In which sentence could *dilemma* fill in the blank?
- Ⓐ Carly wore her beautiful new _____ to a birthday party.
- Ⓑ Let's get together and think of a great _____ for our class project.
- Ⓒ I can only invite one friend to go to Disney World with us. What a _____!
- Ⓓ When you've decided, please give me a _____ so I can make plans.

4. What would someone say if he were *determined* to enter a contest?
- Ⓕ "Shall I enter it, or not? I'm unsure, so I need your advice."
- Ⓖ "I've made up my mind. I'm entering it no matter what!"
- Ⓗ "I'm interested in entering, but I think I'll wait until next year."
- Ⓙ "I can never win that contest, so I won't bother entering it."

Writing

Write about a time when you faced a happy dilemma (when all of your choices were good ones). Use **dilemma** in your sentences.

_____

_____

_____

obligation

noun

something that you must do

synonym: duty

After my birthday, one of my **obligations** was to write thank-you notes to the people who gave me gifts.

Which of the following mean about the same as **obligation**?

- job
- wish
- duty
- punishment
- responsibility

Tell about an **obligation** you have at home. Do you have any **obligations** at school? Do you think it's important to honor your **obligations**? Why?

panic

noun

a sudden feeling of great fear that comes over a person or group of people

verb

to feel or be overcome by **panic**

I felt **panic** when I thought I'd lost my purse. "Don't **panic**!" said my friend. "It's right behind your chair."

Which of these situations might cause **panic**?

- You get a drink of water.
- A building catches on fire.
- A tiger gets loose at the zoo.
- People picnic peacefully at the park.
- You lock yourself out of your house and have left something cooking on the stove.

Have you ever heard someone say "Don't **panic**!"? What was the situation?

lofty

adjective

1. very high
2. grand or noble

Roberta's **lofty** ambitions include designing **lofty** skyscrapers in New York City.

Which of the following could be described as **lofty**?

- the height at which an airplane flies
- a peak in the Rocky Mountains
- the bottom of the ocean
- the top of a hundred-story building
- the floor of our classroom

Have you ever been to a **lofty** place? Where was it? How did you feel up there?

dawdle

verb

to waste time; be slow

If you **dawdle** before breakfast, you'll miss your ride to school.

Complete the graphic organizer for **dawdle**.

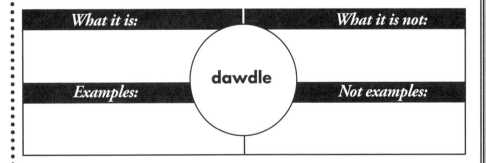

What it is:		*What it is not:*
	dawdle	
Examples:		*Not examples:*

When do you like to **dawdle**? How do you feel when someone else **dawdles** and you're in a hurry?

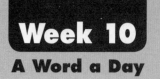
obligation • panic • lofty • dawdle

Write on the board the four words studied this week. Read the words with the class and briefly review their meanings. Then conduct the oral activities below.

1 Tell students that you are going to give them a clue about one of the words for the week. They are to find the word that answers the clue.

- You might feel this when you are very scared. **(panic)**

- If you do this, you might be late for school. **(dawdle)**

- A job is one. **(an obligation)**

- You might use this word to describe a tall treetop. **(lofty)**

2 Read each sentence and ask students to supply the correct word to complete the sentence.

- Mount Everest's ____ peak is the highest spot on Earth. **(lofty)**

- Please don't ____! We'll be late for our appointment. **(dawdle)**

- I promised my friend, so now I have an ____ to go. **(obligation)**

- During the earthquake, Max's first reaction was ____. **(panic)**

3 Read each sentence and ask students to tell which word is wrong. Then have them provide the correct word from the week's list.

- I can see the whole city from the roof of this low building. **(low/lofty)**

- If you promise to complete a project, you have an option to finish the work. **(option/obligation)**

- When a fox got into the chicken house, the chickens were in a state of calm. **(calm/panic)**

- Please don't hurry—your dinner will get cold. **(hurry/dawdle)**

4 Read each sentence and ask students to decide if it is true or false. If the sentence is false, instruct students to explain why.

- The bottom of a deep hole is a lofty place. **(false; a lofty place is high in the air)**

- A little child might feel panic if she got lost in a supermarket. **(true)**

- If you have an obligation to go somewhere, you must go. **(true)**

- Most people dawdle if they think they are going to be late. **(false; most people hurry in that situation)**

Answers for page 43: 1. C, 2. J, 3. A, 4. G

| **Review Words** | obligation • panic • lofty • dawdle |

Fill in the bubble next to the correct answer.

1. **Which word means the opposite of *dawdle*?**
   - Ⓐ stroll
   - Ⓑ wander
   - Ⓒ hurry
   - Ⓓ halt

2. **Which word pair is the opposite of both meanings of *lofty*?**
   - Ⓕ wide, elevated
   - Ⓖ high, impressive
   - Ⓗ thin, important
   - Ⓙ low, ordinary

3. **In which sentence could *panic* fill in the blank?**
   - Ⓐ When a lion chased them, the antelopes felt ____.
   - Ⓑ I was filled with ____ when I found out that I was the winner.
   - Ⓒ Tonight I can't fall asleep, though I usually feel ____ at bedtime.
   - Ⓓ Sometimes my sister messes up my room, filling me with ____.

4. **Which sentence tells about an *obligation*?**
   - Ⓕ You may help with the gardening if you want to.
   - Ⓖ Mowing the lawn is one of Alex's weekly chores.
   - Ⓗ Mom wishes that she had more time for gardening.
   - Ⓙ Mr. Morel has a garden supply store that sells plants.

| **Writing** |

Write about a time when dawdling caused a problem for you. Use **dawdle** in your sentences.

_____

_____

_____

gloomy

adjective

1. dull and dark
2. sad

The **gloomy** weather on the day of the school picnic was mirrored by the **gloomy** expressions on the students' faces.

Which of the following would you describe as **gloomy**?

- pizza day in the cafeteria
- an underground cavern lit only by a candle
- your house when the power goes out at sundown
- the way you feel when you get an A on a test
- the way you feel when your field trip is canceled

What do you do to cheer yourself up when you feel **gloomy**? How can you help cheer up a friend who feels **gloomy**?

ache

noun

a dull, steady pain

After the doctor gave me a shot, I had an **ache** in my arm for a few days.

Which of these might give you an **ache**?

- eating a dozen doughnuts
- having a cavity in your tooth
- falling off your bike
- reading a book
- taking a bath

What makes you feel better when you have an **ache**?

lackadaisical

adjective

lacking interest, enthusiasm, or energy

Your piano playing won't improve if you have a **lackadaisical** attitude about practicing.

Complete the graphic organizer for **lackadaisical**.

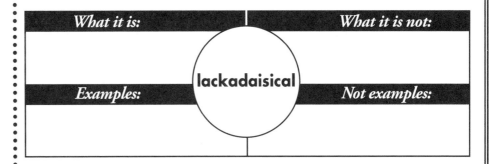

What it is:		What it is not:
	lackadaisical	
Examples:		Not examples:

What is something you feel **lackadaisical** about? Is it a good idea to be **lackadaisical** about your schoolwork? Why or why not?

gossip

verb

to talk about other people's personal lives when they are not present

The neighbors **gossiped** about why the Wong family moved to New York, but no one really knew for sure.

Would you be **gossiping** if you:

- told someone the name of your new dog?
- talked about why you didn't like the new girl in class?
- shared a secret your sister told you about her best friend?
- told a friend the new paint color in your bedroom?
- told a story about someone's parents even though you weren't sure it was true?

What could you say to someone who wants to **gossip** to you about others?

Review

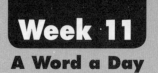

gloomy • ache • lackadaisical • gossip

Write on the board the four words studied this week. Read the words with the class and briefly review their meanings. Then conduct the oral activities below.

1 Tell students that you are going to give them a clue about one of the words for the week. They are to find the word that answers the clue.

- If you eat too much candy, your teeth might develop one of these. **(an ache)**

- When people do this, they talk about other people's personal lives. **(gossip)**

- You might have this kind of attitude about pulling weeds in the flower beds. **(lackadaisical)**

- This word could be used to describe a rainy day. **(gloomy)**

2 Read each sentence and ask students to supply the correct word to complete the sentence.

- After pitching five innings, Ana had an ____ in her arm. **(ache)**

- Ben's ____ attitude about doing his homework resulted in a low math grade. **(lackadaisical)**

- Some people like to ____ about things that happen to movie stars. **(gossip)**

- My ____ mood improved when I heard that Dad was bringing home my favorite food for dinner. **(gloomy)**

3 Read each sentence and ask students to tell which word or words are wrong. Then have them provide the correct word from the week's list.

- Music may cheer you up if you are in a good mood. **(good/gloomy)**

- Don't be so enthusiastic about doing your chores. **(enthusiastic/lackadaisical)**

- Jill kept a secret by telling her classmates that the teacher is getting married. **(kept a secret/gossiped)**

4 Read each sentence and ask students to decide if it is true or false. If the sentence is false, instruct students to explain why.

- People who gossip may spread untrue information. **(true)**

- Surprise parties make most people feel gloomy. **(false; most people feel happy about them)**

- Someone could get muscle aches from lifting heavy items. **(true)**

- Most people feel lackadaisical about doing boring jobs. **(true)**

Answers for page 47: 1. A, 2. J, 3. B, 4. J

gloomy • ache • lackadaisical • gossip

Fill in the bubble next to the correct answer.

1. **Which word means the opposite of *lackadaisical*?**
   Ⓐ enthusiastic
   Ⓑ bored
   Ⓒ puzzled
   Ⓓ exhausted

2. **Which word means the opposite of *gloomy*?**
   Ⓕ angry
   Ⓖ bored
   Ⓗ sorrowful
   Ⓙ cheerful

3. **In which sentence could *gossip* fill in the blank?**
   Ⓐ The company directors meet to ____ about important business.
   Ⓑ My sister and her friend ____ about their classmates on the phone.
   Ⓒ Whenever I have a problem, I ____ about it with my mom or dad.
   Ⓓ On TV news programs, newscasters ____ about current events.

4. **In which sentence could *ache* fill in the blank?**
   Ⓕ I have an ____ in my shoe. Please wait while I get it out.
   Ⓖ There is an ____ in this soup that makes it taste salty.
   Ⓗ An ____ runs through the valley between the mountains.
   Ⓙ After gymnastics class, Emma had an ____ in her knee.

Writing

Write about something you feel lackadaisical about. Use **lackadaisical** in your sentences.

_____

_____

_____

mischief

noun

playful behavior that often annoys or irritates others and may cause harm

The puppies' **mischief** stopped being funny when they chewed up Papi's new slippers.

Which of the following are examples of **mischief**?

- hiding a book from your friend
- doing the dishes without being asked
- tying your friend's shoelaces together
- giving your mother a rose on Mother's Day
- having a pillow fight and getting feathers all over the room

Do you like making **mischief**? How do you feel when someone else makes **mischief**?

moist

adjective

slightly wet or damp

I used a **moist** towel to wipe the pencil marks off my desk.

Complete the graphic organizer for **moist**.

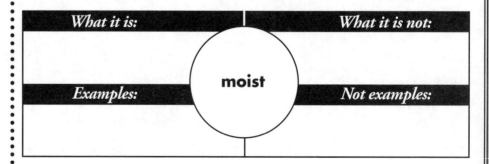

What it is:	*What it is not:*
moist	
Examples:	*Not examples:*

How many ways can you think of to make something **moist**?

adapt

verb

to change in order to get along in a new situation

synonym: adjust

A chameleon can **adapt** to its surroundings by changing color to blend in with rocks and trees.

In which of the following situations would you need to **adapt**?

- moving to a new school at the beginning of the year
- waking up in the same house every day
- having an ice-cream sundae for dessert
- having a new baby in the family
- breaking a leg

Do you **adapt** easily to new situations, or is it hard for you to **adapt**? What helps you to **adapt** and feel comfortable in a new situation?

habitat

noun

the home of a particular group of plants and animals

Although you might see a lion at a wild animal park, its natural **habitat** is the African savanna.

What is the natural **habitat** of each of the following?

- ferns
- deer
- seaweed
- polar bears
- howler monkeys

What kind of **habitat** would you like to visit? Where is it?

Review

mischief • moist • adapt • habitat

Write on the board the four words studied this week. Read the words with the class and briefly review their meanings. Then conduct the oral activities below.

❶ Tell students that you are going to give them a clue about one of the words for the week. They are to find the word that answers the clue.

- A desert is one. A rainforest is another. (**habitat**)

- You might use this word to describe a nervous person's sweaty hands. (**moist**)

- This kind of behavior can be annoying. (**mischief**)

- When you begin a new grade at school or move to a new home, you must do this. (**adapt to it**)

❷ Read each sentence and ask students to supply the correct word to complete the sentence.

- Small, colorful frogs live in a rainforest _____. (**habitat**)

- The grass is still _____ from yesterday's rainfall. (**moist**)

- Our baby sitter makes sure that we don't get into _____ while our mom is at work. (**mischief**)

- Arctic foxes can _____ to snowy surroundings. Their fur turns white in the wintertime. (**adapt**)

❸ Read each list of words and phrases. Ask students to supply the word that fits best with each.

- adjust to change, get used to a new home, fit in (**adapt**)

- natural home, surroundings, ecosystem (**habitat**)

- misbehavior, shenanigans, annoying acts (**mischief**)

- wet, damp, almost dry (**moist**)

❹ Read each sentence and ask students to decide if it is true or false. If the sentence is false, instruct students to explain why.

- Getting into mischief isn't as bad as breaking the law. (**true**)

- Grass is often moist in the early morning. (**true**)

- A polar bear's thick white fur is its habitat. (**false; its cold, snowy home is its habitat**)

- Refusing to change helps people adapt to different situations. (**false; being flexible helps people adapt to different situations**)

Answers for page 51: 1. D, 2. H, 3. A, 4. G

Name _____

Fill in the bubble next to the correct answer.

1. **Which word means the opposite of *moist*?**

   Ⓐ damp

   Ⓑ cracked

   Ⓒ slimy

   Ⓓ dry

2. **Which word has about the same meaning as *mischief*?**

   Ⓕ misuse

   Ⓖ mistake

   Ⓗ misbehavior

   Ⓙ misunderstanding

3. **In which sentence could *habitat* fill in the blank?**

   Ⓐ Tall cactus plants live in this desert ____.

   Ⓑ Shelby is wearing a pink and white ____ today.

   Ⓒ Our family's ____ is located at 2145 Basil Lane.

   Ⓓ This ____ tastes delicious. Did your mom make it?

4. **How could a child *adapt* to a new neighborhood?**

   Ⓕ by moving away from home

   Ⓖ by making new friends

   Ⓗ by packing a suitcase

   Ⓙ by saying goodbye to old friends

Writing

Write about a time when you had to adapt to a new situation. Use **adapt** in your sentences.

_____

_____

drenched

adjective

soaked or
completely wet

We got **drenched** when we were caught out in the rain without an umbrella.

Complete the graphic organizer for **drenched**.

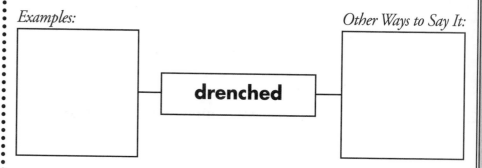

Examples:

drenched

Other Ways to Say It:

Tell about a time when you got **drenched**. Was it fun? Did you get cold, or was it a hot day? Was it an accident or on purpose?

absorb

verb

1. to soak up liquid
2. to take in information

I read the instructions twice in order to **absorb** the information about how to **absorb** the paint I spilled on the rug.

Which of the following could you **absorb** with a sponge?

- the water in a fish tank
- a mud puddle in your backyard
- water left on the floor after your shower
- grape juice that spilled on the cafeteria floor
- ice cream that melted on the kitchen counter

For what topics do you find it easy to **absorb** information? For what topics do you find it hard to **absorb** information?

legend

noun

a story that is handed down from the past that is often based on fact, but is not completely true

The **legend** of Johnny Appleseed is based on the life of a man named John Chapman.

Which of these is probably a **legend**?

- People lived without electricity in the past.
- My great-uncle Sam could eat fifty pies in one sitting.
- We had a one-legged dog that could run faster than a train.
- My grandmother once stayed up for four days straight sewing a quilt.
- Early settlers crossed the United States in wagons.

If you could have a **legend** passed down about you, what would you like people to say?

glitter

verb

to shine and sparkle

The crystal goblets are so clean that they **glitter** in the candlelight.

Which of the following **glitter**?

- a tennis shoe
- a diamond ring
- the stars at night
- jewels in a crown
- a peanut butter sandwich

What is something you own that **glitters**?

Review

drenched • absorb • legend • glitter

Write on the board the four words studied this week. Read the words with the class and briefly review their meanings. Then conduct the oral activities below.

1 Tell students that you are going to give them a clue about one of the words for the week. They are to find the word that answers the clue.

- A dry sponge does this to water. **(absorbs it)**

- Diamonds and other jewels do this in the sunlight. **(glitter)**

- The story of John Henry is one. **(a legend)**

- Imagine that you have just splashed through a deep puddle. You could use this word to describe your feet, shoes, and socks. **(drenched)**

2 Read each sentence and ask students to supply the correct word to complete the sentence.

- Plants ____ moisture through their roots. **(absorb)**

- A town ____ says that buried treasure lies beneath that old house. **(legend)**

- Peering into a cave, I saw an animal's eyes ____. **(glitter)**

- When the cat came in out of the rain, his fur was completely ____. **(drenched)**

3 Read each list of words and phrases. Ask students to supply the word that fits best with each.

- sparkle, shine, diamonds, rubies, emeralds **(glitter)**

- soak up, sponge, take in, learn **(absorb)**

- soaked to the skin, wet through and through **(drenched)**

- old story, traditional tale, passed down through generations **(legend)**

4 Read each sentence and ask students to decide if it is true or false. If the sentence is false, instruct students to explain why.

- A legend is exactly the same as a fairy tale. **(false; most legends are based on real events)**

- A scientist must absorb a lot of information in his or her subject area. **(true)**

- *Drenched* and *damp* have the same meaning. **(false; *drenched* means *soaking wet* and *damp* means *slightly wet*)**

- Shiny new cars glitter. **(true)**

Answers for page 55: 1. D, 2. F, 3. B, 4. F

Name _____

Fill in the bubble next to the correct answer.

1. **Which word means the opposite of *drenched*?**
   - Ⓐ soaked
   - Ⓑ open
   - Ⓒ closed
   - Ⓓ dry

2. **Which word has about the same meaning as *glitter*?**
   - Ⓕ sparkle
   - Ⓖ snarl
   - Ⓗ chatter
   - Ⓙ twitch

3. **In which sentence could *absorb* fill in the blank?**
   - Ⓐ Use a large wooden spoon to ____ the soup.
   - Ⓑ The yard flooded because the dirt couldn't ____ the rainfall.
   - Ⓒ The tree fell over because it couldn't ____ the strong winds.
   - Ⓓ I sometimes use a drinking straw to ____ juice from a glass.

4. **Which of these is a *legend*?**
   - Ⓕ George Washington chopping down a cherry tree
   - Ⓖ a newspaper story about a presidential election
   - Ⓗ a fictional book about a fourth-grader and his friends
   - Ⓙ an instruction book that tells how to use a computer

Writing

Write about an interesting way to get dry if you are drenched. Use **drenched** in your sentences.

_____

_____

_____

amuse

verb

to make someone laugh or smile

The playful monkeys always **amuse** the visitors at the zoo.

Which of the following would **amuse** you?

- your new puppy licks your hand
- a magician finds a coin behind your ear
- someone accidentally steps on your toe
- a clown squirts water from a flower pinned to his coat
- your milk spills in your lunch and ruins your sandwich

Tell about a time when someone did something that **amused** you. What is something that you have done to **amuse** others?

weary

adjective

tired or exhausted

Mom was **weary** after driving for almost three days to get to Grandma's house.

Complete the graphic organizer for **weary**.

Examples:

Other Ways to Say It:

weary

What makes you feel **weary**? What can you do to feel better when you're feeling **weary**?

baffled

adjective

confused or puzzled

synonym: perplexed

I was **baffled** by the complicated directions for assembling my new model car.

Which of the following might leave you **baffled**?

- buttoning your shirt
- assembling a puzzle with 10,000 pieces
- trying to read something in a foreign language
- figuring out which end of the pencil has the eraser
- following directions for folding a piece of paper into the shape of a bird

When you are feeling **baffled** by a task, what resources can you turn to?

marionette

noun

a puppet that is moved by pulling strings or wires attached to parts of its body

The puppeteer was so skilled in moving the **marionette** that the puppet almost seemed real.

Which of these describes a **marionette**?

- can be made by hand
- can really walk and talk
- needs a person in order to move
- can be dressed in cute clothing
- can feel sad if people don't like the show

If you had a magical **marionette** that could come to life, what sort of **marionette** would it be?

amuse • weary • baffled • marionette

Write on the board the four words studied this week. Read the words with the class and briefly review their meanings. Then conduct the oral activities below.

1 Tell students that you are going to give them a clue about one of the words for the week. They are to find the word that answers the clue.

- This is a kind of puppet. (**a marionette**)

- You would feel this way if you took a long hike up a steep mountain trail. (**weary**)

- A comedian gets paid to do this. (**amuse people**)

- You might feel this way if someone spoke to you in a language that you didn't understand. (**baffled**)

2 Read each sentence and ask students to supply the correct word to complete the sentence.

- Everyone felt ____ by the difficult math problem. Not even the teacher could solve it. (**baffled**)

- Taylor felt ____ after a long gymnastics workout. (**weary**)

- Kittens ____ me when they chase their own tails. (**amuse**)

- The puppeteer made the ____ dance by pulling its strings. (**marionette**)

3 Read each list of words and phrases. Ask students to supply the word that fits best with each.

- confused, puzzled, bewildered, perplexed (**baffled**)

- wooden, strings or wires, puppet, Pinocchio (**marionette**)

- make people laugh, entertain, delight (**amuse**)

- tired, exhausted, ready for bed (**weary**)

4 Read each sentence and ask students to decide if it is true or false. If the sentence is false, instruct students to explain why.

- *Weary* and *exhausted* are synonyms. (**true**)

- You might amuse people by telling them jokes. (**true**)

- If you solved a word puzzle, you would probably feel baffled. (**false; you would feel baffled if you *couldn't* solve the puzzle**)

- You move a marionette by pushing a button. (**false; you move it by pulling its strings**)

Answers for page 59: 1. C, 2. H, 3. C, 4. J

Review Words   amuse • weary • baffled • marionette

Fill in the bubble next to the correct answer.

1. **Which word means the opposite of *weary*?**
   Ⓐ trusting
   Ⓑ thankful
   Ⓒ energetic
   Ⓓ exhausted

2. **Which word has about the same meaning as *baffled*?**
   Ⓕ enchanted
   Ⓖ interested
   Ⓗ confused
   Ⓙ angry

3. **Which sentence correctly uses the word *amuse*?**
   Ⓐ The terrible news will amuse everyone who hears it.
   Ⓑ Amuse yourself by finishing your homework before bedtime.
   Ⓒ I sent Eva a funny card because I knew it would amuse her.
   Ⓓ Please amuse me—I didn't mean to bump into you like that.

4. **Which of these story characters is a *marionette*?**
   Ⓕ Goldilocks
   Ⓖ the Gingerbread Boy
   Ⓗ the Big Bad Wolf
   Ⓙ Pinocchio

Writing

Write about the last time you felt weary. What caused you to feel that way?
Use **weary** in your sentences.

_____

_____

_____

command

verb

to order someone to do something

The trainer at the wild animal park **commanded** the wolf to bring him a stick.

Which of the following might you say if you were **commanding** someone?

- "Go away!"
- "Come here!"
- "That's a nice shirt!"
- "May I borrow your pencil?"
- "Give me that right now!"

Do you like it when someone **commands** you to do something? Is there a time when it's necessary to **command** others?

hilarious

adjective

very funny

synonym: hysterical

The movie was so **hilarious** that we almost cried from laughing so hard.

Which of the following might be **hilarious**?

- changing a light bulb
- a clown at the circus
- watching bread dough rise
- a book of knock-knock jokes
- a puppy chasing its tail

Tell about something **hilarious** that made you laugh.

devour

verb

to eat something very quickly or hungrily

Zoo visitors like to gather at feeding time to watch the cheetahs **devour** their steak.

Complete the graphic organizer for **devour**.

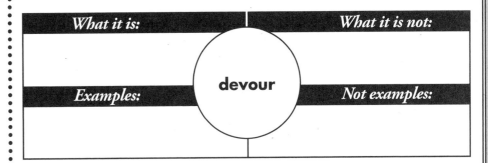

Have you ever **devoured** some food? If so, what were you eating? Did you enjoy it?

solo

noun

a performance by one performer

You could tell that Anoki had been practicing, because he performed his **solo** perfectly.

Which of the following describe a **solo**?

- keeping the beat on a drum while your classmates march
- playing the piano all by yourself at a concert
- singing a song alone as part of a play
- playing on a baseball team
- singing in a choir

Have you ever performed a **solo**? How did you feel, or how do you think you would feel?

command • hilarious • devour • solo

Write on the board the four words studied this week. Read the words with the class and briefly review their meanings. Then conduct the oral activities below.

1 Tell students that you are going to give them a clue about one of the words for the week. They are to find the word that answers the clue.

- This is a one-person performance. **(a solo)**

- You do this when you tell a dog, "Sit!" **(command it)**

- Wolves do this to their prey. **(devour it)**

- You might use this word to describe a comedian's act. **(hilarious)**

2 Read each sentence and ask students to supply the correct word to complete the sentence.

- The musician performed a beautiful violin ____. **(solo)**

- "I ____ you to halt!" said the starship captain. **(command)**

- Please don't ____ your dinner like a wild animal. Eat more slowly and politely. **(devour)**

- I couldn't stop laughing at Stan's ____ jokes. **(hilarious)**

3 Read each sentence and ask students to tell which word or words are wrong. Then have them provide the correct word from the week's list.

- The look on Anna's face was so frightening that it made me laugh. **(frightening/hilarious)**

- I sang a duet for the audience all by myself. **(duet/solo)**

- "Stop making excuses and clean your room immediately!" Mom suggested. **(suggested/commanded)**

- I'm so hungry in the morning that I pick at my breakfast. **(pick at/devour)**

4 Read each sentence and ask students to decide if it is true or false. If the sentence is false, instruct students to explain why.

- Three singers perform a solo together. **(false; a single singer performs a solo)**

- Diners at fancy restaurants usually devour their food. **(false; they usually eat slowly and politely)**

- It is part of an army officer's job to command soldiers. **(true)**

- Filmmakers who make comedies hope that their movies will be hilarious. **(true)**

Answers for page 63: 1. D, 2. G, 3. B, 4. H

Review Words command • hilarious • devour • solo

Fill in the bubble next to the correct answer.

1. **Which word has the same meaning as *command*?**
   Ⓐ beg
   Ⓑ inquire
   Ⓒ request
   Ⓓ order

2. **Which word has about the same meaning as *devour*?**
   Ⓕ nibble
   Ⓖ gobble
   Ⓗ taste
   Ⓙ digest

3. **Which sentence correctly uses the word *solo*?**
   Ⓐ At the wedding, four guests sang a solo of "Wedding Bell Blues."
   Ⓑ I felt nervous as I sang my solo, but my voice sounded okay.
   Ⓒ A small orchestra performed a solo to open the concert.
   Ⓓ My cousin and I performed a piano solo together.

4. **Which of these is supposed to be *hilarious*?**
   Ⓕ climbing a tall mountain
   Ⓖ breakfast on a weekday
   Ⓗ a comedy show on TV
   Ⓙ a math lesson in school

Writing

Write about something funny you have seen. Use **hilarious** in your sentences.

_____

_____

_____

unique

adjective

someone or something that is the only one of its kind

A fish that could survive on dry land would be **unique**.

Which of the following are **unique**?

- white tennis shoes
- a lunchbox just like your best friend's
- a planet scientists have never seen before
- the only baseball card ever made of a certain player
- being the only student in the school that has never been absent

What is something about you that is **unique**? What is something **unique** about someone in your family?

candidate

noun

someone who is applying for a job or running in an election

Each **candidate** for school president gave a speech at the assembly.

Which of the following are **candidates**?

- the new bus driver
- five people applying for a job
- a new cook at your favorite restaurant
- the people running for president of the United States
- a teacher who visits the school to decide if she wants to accept a job there

Do you think you would ever like to be a **candidate** in an election? Why or why not?

numerous

adjective

many; great in number

The curious student asked **numerous** questions during the science lesson.

Complete the graphic organizer for **numerous**.

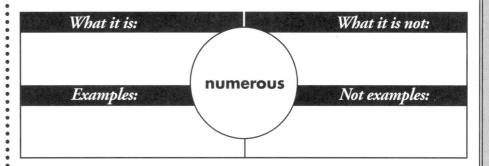

What it is:	*What it is not:*
Examples:	*Not examples:*

Do you think it's better to have **numerous** friends or **numerous** things? Why?

exact

adjective

correct; having no mistakes

We need to know the **exact** measurements of the desk to be sure it will fit in my room.

Is it important to be **exact** about:

- the letters in words that you spell?
- the time of your dental appointment?
- the change you get back when you buy groceries?
- the number of leaves on the tree in your yard?
- how many times you blink your eyes each day?

What is something that you are careful to be **exact** about? Why is it important to you?

unique • candidate • numerous • exact

Write on the board the four words studied this week. Read the words with the class and briefly review their meanings. Then conduct the oral activities below.

1 Tell students that you are going to give them a clue about one of the words for the week. They are to find the word that answers the clue.

- You might use this word to describe ants in an anthill. **(numerous)**

- When giving your address, you need to provide these kinds of numbers. **(exact)**

- Since you are different from everyone else in the world, this word describes you. **(unique)**

- In 2008 Hillary Clinton was one. She was running for the U.S. presidency. **(a candidate)**

2 Read each sentence and ask students to supply the correct word to complete the sentence.

- Pablo is a ____ for captain of the soccer team. **(candidate)**

- The ____ time is 2:17 in the afternoon. **(exact)**

- The party guests were so ____ that I didn't get a chance to meet them all. **(numerous)**

- The five sisters look a lot alike, but each has ____ traits that make her stand out. **(unique)**

3 Read each sentence and ask students to tell which word or words are wrong. Then have them provide the correct word from the week's list.

- Only a few bees live in each hive. **(Only a few/Numerous)**

- I know the approximate number of pennies in this jar: 879. **(approximate/exact)**

- Each person in the world is just like everyone else. **(just like everyone else/unique)**

4 Read each sentence and ask students to decide if it is true or false. If the sentence is false, instruct students to explain why.

- "Between 20 and 30" is not an exact number. **(true)**

- In many cities, pigeons are numerous. **(true)**

- Your unique qualities are those that no one else has. **(true)**

- A candidate is a person who wins an election. **(false; some candidates win, but others lose)**

Answers for page 67: 1. B, 2. J, 3. D, 4. F

A Word a Day • EMC 2794 • © Evan-Moor Corp.

Review Words | unique • candidate • numerous • exact

Fill in the bubble next to the correct answer.

1. **Which word means the opposite of *numerous*?**
   Ⓐ simple
   Ⓑ few
   Ⓒ many
   Ⓓ complicated

2. **Which phrase has the same meaning as *unique*?**
   Ⓕ like bumps on a log
   Ⓖ a dime a dozen
   Ⓗ two peas in a pod
   Ⓙ one of a kind

3. **Which sentence correctly uses the word *exact*?**
   Ⓐ The exact amount I have in my bank account is about $20.
   Ⓑ My exact weight is about ten pounds more than a year ago.
   Ⓒ The exact number of wedding guests is between 100 and 150.
   Ⓓ In exact numbers, the shelter has room for 37 dogs and 42 cats.

4. **What is a presidential *candidate*?**
   Ⓕ someone who runs for president
   Ⓖ someone who votes in an election
   Ⓗ someone who likes the president
   Ⓙ someone who works for the president

Writing

Write about something you'd like to do in your life that would be unique in the world. Use **unique** in your sentences.

_____

_____

_____

digits

noun

1. the numerals from zero through nine
2. fingers and toes

We have started adding numbers with three **digits** in math this week.

Which of the following include **digits**?

- your phone number
- your birth date
- your hands
- your name
- your age

How many **digits** do you have on one hand? How many **digits** do you have altogether?

shrub

noun

a plant that has several woody stems instead of a trunk

synonym: bush

The yard looked beautiful now that several of the **shrubs** were blooming.

Where might you see a **shrub**?

- around a house
- in the cafeteria
- at a garden shop
- in the principal's office
- at a park

Can you name any **shrubs** that you have around your home? Do they ever bloom? When?

luminous

adjective

giving off light

The full moon was so **luminous** that Tim did not need a flashlight to see the path.

Which of these manufactured objects are **luminous**?

- a burning candle
- a fountain
- a fluorescent light
- a telephone
- a flashing camera

What are some **luminous** objects that are found in nature?

belligerent

adjective

hostile; wanting to fight

The Peacemakers at our school use conflict resolution to help stop **belligerent** behavior.

Complete the graphic organizer for **belligerent**.

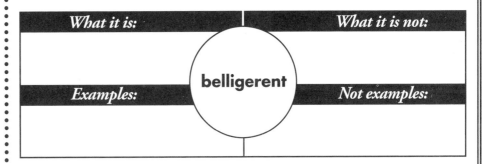

How do you feel when someone becomes **belligerent**? What do you do? What situations make you feel **belligerent**? How do you handle those situations?

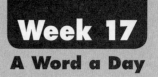

digits • shrub • luminous • belligerent

Write on the board the four words studied this week. Read the words with the class and briefly review their meanings. Then conduct the oral activities below.

1 Tell students that you are going to give them a clue about one of the words for the week. They are to find the word that answers the clue.

- You might use this word to describe a cat's eyes glowing in the dark. **(luminous)**

- You might use this word to describe a bully. **(belligerent)**

- You might have these growing around the base of your home. **(shrubs)**

- A local phone number has seven of these in it. **(digits)**

2 Read each sentence and ask students to supply the correct word to complete the sentence.

- Let's plant a flowering ____ next to the front porch. **(shrub)**

- I peered through the darkness at my ____ clock dial and saw that it was midnight. **(luminous)**

- One ____ student started a fight in the cafeteria. **(belligerent)**

- Our car's license plate has three letters and three ____. **(digits)**

3 Read each sentence and ask students to tell which word is wrong. Then have them provide the correct word from the week's list.

- A phone number has ten letters, including the area code: (510) 555-1617. **(letters/digits)**

- A friendly grizzly bear charged Joel, who escaped just in time. **(friendly/belligerent)**

- A dark full moon lit our way through the darkness. **(dark/luminous)**

- My ball rolled under the branches of the small bench next to the driveway. **(bench/shrub)**

4 Read each sentence and ask students to decide if it is true or false. If the sentence is false, instruct students to explain why.

- Neon signs look luminous in the dark. **(true)**

- Shrubs are taller than most trees. **(false; they are shorter)**

- A teenager's age has one digit. **(false; it has two digits: 13, 14, 15, 16, and so on)**

- Behaving in a belligerent way helps people to settle their arguments peacefully. **(false; belligerent behavior can result in physical fights)**

Answers for page 71: 1. C, 2. H, 3. B, 4. H

| **Review Words** | digits • shrub • luminous • belligerent |

Fill in the bubble next to the correct answer.

1. **Which word means the opposite of *belligerent*?**
   Ⓐ angry
   Ⓑ intelligent
   Ⓒ friendly
   Ⓓ uneducated

2. **Which are *digits*?**
   Ⓕ ABCDEFGHIJK
   Ⓖ + = & % $
   Ⓗ 0123456789
   Ⓙ { } [ ] ( ) < >

3. **Which word has the same meaning as *luminous*?**
   Ⓐ smooth
   Ⓑ glowing
   Ⓒ slimy
   Ⓓ curving

4. **Which is true of a *shrub*?**
   Ⓕ It is a small mammal.
   Ⓖ It is a tall pine tree.
   Ⓗ It could be called a bush.
   Ⓙ It is a large reptile.

| **Writing** |

Write about how you would act if you encountered a belligerent person.
Use **belligerent** in your sentences.

_____

_____

_____

elated

adjective

filled with joy

antonym: miserable

Jessica felt **elated** when she crossed the finish line first.

Which of these might you do if you felt **elated**?

- sleep
- jump up and down
- cheer
- yawn
- grin broadly

Tell about some events in your life that made you feel **elated**.

deceive

verb

to make someone believe something that is not true; to trick

synonym: lie

The wolf tried to **deceive** Little Red Riding Hood by dressing like her grandmother.

Which words mean about the same as **deceive**?

- mislead
- verify
- confirm
- falsify
- receive

Did anyone ever **deceive** you? How did it make you feel? Do you think it's ever OK to **deceive** someone else?

absurd

adjective

without good sense

synonym: silly

It was **absurd** to try to eat the broth with a fork!

Complete the graphic organizer for **absurd**.

Examples:

absurd

Other Ways to Say It:

What is the most **absurd** thing you have ever seen or heard?

vanquish

verb

to defeat; overcome

synonym: conquer

Zack had to **vanquish** his fear of the dark before going camping with his friends.

Which scenarios describe somebody **vanquishing** someone or something?

- two runners cross the finish line at the same moment
- a tennis player beats her opponent in every game
- a person with a learning disability gets all As
- a baseball team finishes the season in last place
- a knight knocks the other rider off his horse in a jousting match

What are some fears you would like to **vanquish**? Why?

elated • deceive • absurd • vanquish

Write on the board the four words studied this week. Read the words with the class and briefly review their meanings. Then conduct the oral activities below.

1 Tell students that you are going to give them a clue about one of the words for the week. They are to find the word that answers the clue.

- You might use this word to describe a silly rhyme. **(absurd)**

- At the end of most fantasy stories, the good guys do this to the bad guys. **(vanquish them)**

- A person does this when he or she tells a lie. **(deceives someone else)**

- You might feel this way if you won a contest. **(elated)**

2 Read each sentence and ask students to supply the correct word to complete the sentence.

- Don't try to ____ me. I can tell that you're lying. **(deceive)**

- "Tomorrow we will ____ our enemy!" the commander told his soldiers. **(vanquish)**

- Don't be ____ ! There are no monsters living in your closet. **(absurd)**

- I felt ____ when I remembered that my favorite cousin was coming to visit. **(elated)**

3 Read each sentence and ask students to tell which word or words are wrong. Then have them provide the correct word from the week's list.

- When my team won I felt so miserable that I yelled with joy. **(miserable/elated)**

- Drivers' licenses for ten-year-olds? That idea is absolutely reasonable! **(reasonable/absurd)**

- Tennis players want to lose to their opponents. **(lose to/vanquish)**

4 Read each sentence and ask students to decide if it is true or false. If the sentence is false, instruct students to explain why.

- Spies often wear disguises in order to deceive others. **(true)**

- Most people feel elated at weddings. **(true)**

- *Absurd* and *nonsensical* are synonyms. **(true)**

- *Vanquish* and *surrender* are synonyms. **(false; they are antonyms)**

Answers for page 75: 1. D, 2. G, 3. A, 4. F

Review Words elated • deceive • absurd • vanquish

Fill in the bubble next to the correct answer.

1. **Which word is a synonym for _vanquish_?**
   Ⓐ challenge
   Ⓑ surrender
   Ⓒ struggle
   Ⓓ defeat

2. **Which word is an antonym for _absurd_?**
   Ⓕ silly
   Ⓖ sensible
   Ⓗ plump
   Ⓙ slender

3. **Which word is an antonym for _elated_?**
   Ⓐ sorrowful
   Ⓑ joyous
   Ⓒ full
   Ⓓ empty

4. **Which is a name for people who _deceive_ others?**
   Ⓕ liars
   Ⓖ robbers
   Ⓗ comedians
   Ⓙ protectors

Writing

Write about a celebration. Use **elated** in your sentences.

_____

_____

_____

remedy

noun

a medicine or treatment used for healing

verb

to return something to its proper condition

Adam's mother gave him mint tea as a **remedy** for his upset stomach. She hoped it would **remedy** his stomachache quickly.

Complete the graphic organizer for **remedy**.

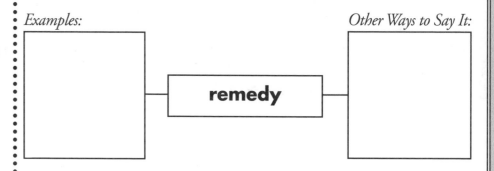

Examples: *Other Ways to Say It:*

remedy

What kind of **remedies** does your family use?
What conditions do you try to **remedy** with them?

bedlam

noun

a scene of noise and confusion

synonym: chaos

There was **bedlam** on the decks of the *Titanic* when the ship began to sink.

Which of these events might cause **bedlam**?

- an earthquake destroys a neighborhood
- a snake gets loose in the classroom
- a bouquet of flowers is delivered
- a fire hydrant floods a city street
- a poet reads one of her poems at a bookstore

Imagine a scene of **bedlam**. Describe what is happening and what caused it.

casual

adjective

1. happening by chance; not planned
2. informal; not fancy

When Jared's **casual** meeting with a friend led to a dinner invitation, he was glad his **casual** clothes were neat and clean.

Which of these scenarios describes a **casual** event or situation?

- Roberto ran into Peter at the park, and they decided to ride their bikes to the shopping center.
- The charity club put on an elaborate dinner served on fine china and linen tablecloths.
- The whole family worked for months to plan their summer holiday.
- Let's just grab a sandwich on the way to the beach.
- Mom and her friend chatted about what had happened during the week.

What kinds of **casual** clothes do you own? Do you like to wear them? Why or why not?

cantankerous

adjective

hard to get along with

synonym: cranky

Because Jerry is so **cantankerous**, I already know he won't agree with me.

Which words describe a person who is **cantankerous**?

- snappy
- agreeable
- crabby
- pleasant
- grouchy

What type of behavior might Jerry have displayed? How do you feel when you are around a **cantankerous** person?

remedy • bedlam • casual • cantankerous

Write on the board the four words studied this week. Read the words with the class and briefly review their meanings. Then conduct the oral activities below.

1 Tell students that you are going to give them a clue about one of the words for the week. They are to find the word that answers the clue.

- This word describes clothing that isn't fancy. **(casual)**

- You would need one if a poisonous snake bit you. **(a remedy)**

- When someone acts this way, it's unpleasant to be around him or her. **(cantankerous)**

- This word names the situation in New York City on September 11, 2001. **(bedlam)**

2 Read each sentence and ask students to supply the correct word to complete the sentence.

- There was ____ in the theater when someone yelled "fire!" **(bedlam)**

- After our ____ meeting at the grocery store, we took a walk together. **(casual)**

- I know you are in a bad mood, but please don't be ____ with your friends. **(cantankerous)**

- Help! Can you do anything to ____ this situation? **(remedy)**

3 Read each sentence and ask students to tell which word is wrong. Then have them provide the correct word from the week's list.

- The cheerful boy snapped at his friend. **(cheerful/cantankerous)**

- We'll be playing outdoors, so be sure to wear formal clothes. **(formal/casual)**

- Following the massive earthquake there was calm throughout the city. **(calm/bedlam)**

4 Read each sentence and ask students to decide if it is true or false. If the sentence is false, instruct students to explain why.

- Medicines may help to remedy people's illnesses. **(true)**

- Bedlam often occurs following a major disaster. **(true)**

- It's a pleasure to talk with cantankerous people. **(false; it's not fun to talk with grouches)**

- *Casual* and *planned* are synonyms. **(false; they are antonyms)**

Answers for page 79: 1. D, 2. G, 3. A, 4. F

Review Words   remedy • bedlam • casual • cantankerous

Fill in the bubble next to the correct answer.

1. **Which word is a synonym for *cantankerous*?**
   Ⓐ concerned
   Ⓑ helpful
   Ⓒ pleasant
   Ⓓ grouchy

2. **Which word is an antonym for *bedlam*?**
   Ⓕ confusion
   Ⓖ peace
   Ⓗ sadness
   Ⓙ industry

3. **Which word is an antonym for *casual*?**
   Ⓐ formal
   Ⓑ tidy
   Ⓒ sloppy
   Ⓓ ordinary

4. **Someone might need a *remedy* in order to _____.**
   Ⓕ heal an illness
   Ⓖ drive a car
   Ⓗ solve a math problem
   Ⓙ climb a tree

Writing

Write about a time when you were cranky. Use **cantankerous** in your sentences.

_____

_____

_____

affluent

adjective

having a lot of money

synonym: wealthy

Marta loved to visit her **affluent** aunt because she had a swimming pool and a tennis court.

Which words mean about the same as **affluent**?

- poor
- rich
- broke
- well-off
- desperate

If you were **affluent**, what special things might you own? How might you help others if you were **affluent**?

hermit

noun

a person who lives alone to be away from other people

synonym: recluse

The **hermit** saw other people only when he hiked into town to buy groceries.

Which of these actions would be likely of a **hermit**?

- to not answer a knock on the door
- to dance for hours at a party
- to list his phone number in the telephone book
- to grow his own food so he didn't have to go to a store
- to not want to make new friends

Why might somebody choose to be a **hermit**? Do you think you would like to be a **hermit**? Why or why not?

A Word a Day • EMC 2794 • © Evan-Moor Corp.

dapper

adjective

attractive in dress

synonym: fashionable

James was such a **dapper** dresser that he looked like a model.

Complete the graphic organizer for **dapper**.

Examples:

dapper

Other Ways to Say It:

Think of famous people who are **dapper** dressers. Which would you most want to dress like?

abscond

verb

to run away suddenly and secretly

The bank robbers planned to **abscond** with thousands of dollars.

Which words or phrases mean about the same as **abscond**?

- escape
- flee
- hightail it
- visit
- bolt

If you planned to **abscond**, where would you go?

Review

affluent • hermit • dapper • abscond

Write on the board the four words studied this week. Read the words with the class and briefly review their meanings. Then conduct the oral activities below.

1 Tell students that you are going to give them a clue about one of the words for the week. They are to find the word that answers the clue.

- Robbers do this with the items they steal. **(abscond with them)**

- This word describes someone with a large bank account. **(affluent)**

- You could use this word to describe a man who's wearing stylish clothes. **(dapper)**

- This person doesn't like being around other people. **(a hermit)**

2 Read each sentence and ask students to supply the correct word to complete the sentence.

- The twins often ____ with forbidden cookies. **(abscond)**

- Pablo looked ____ at the wedding in his stylish new clothes. **(dapper)**

- Deep in the woods lived an old ____ with a long beard. **(hermit)**

- The ____ businesswoman gave thousands of dollars to charity. **(affluent)**

3 Read each sentence and ask students to tell which word or words are wrong. Then have them provide the correct word from the week's list.

- The poor family has a beautiful new swimming pool in their backyard. **(poor/affluent)**

- Thieves usually bring back the items they steal. **(bring back/abscond with)**

- Max looks sloppy in his trendy new clothes. **(sloppy/dapper)**

- The socialite lived in a tiny cottage many miles from town. **(socialite/hermit)**

4 Read each sentence and ask students to decide if it is true or false. If the sentence is false, instruct students to explain why.

- A hermit would hate to live in a crowded city. **(true)**

- Most people want to look dapper at fancy events. **(true)**

- Affluent people can afford to eat in expensive restaurants. **(true)**

- It is illegal to abscond with other people's money. **(true)**

Answers for page 83: 1. A, 2. H, 3. C, 4. G

Name _____

Review Words   affluent • hermit • dapper • abscond

Fill in the bubble next to the correct answer.

1. **Which word is a synonym for *dapper*?**
   - Ⓐ stylish
   - Ⓑ casual
   - Ⓒ unattractive
   - Ⓓ unique

2. **Which word is an antonym for *affluent*?**
   - Ⓕ friendly
   - Ⓖ charitable
   - Ⓗ needy
   - Ⓙ uneducated

3. **In which sentence is the word *hermit* used correctly?**
   - Ⓐ Every week the hermit throws a big party for all his friends.
   - Ⓑ The audience clapped after the hermit finished telling jokes.
   - Ⓒ The hermit ignored his relatives' requests to visit him.
   - Ⓓ A hermit will star in the new reality show *Find Me If You Can*.

4. **With which of these might a mouse *abscond*?**
   - Ⓕ a cat
   - Ⓖ some cheese
   - Ⓗ its tail
   - Ⓙ a nest in an attic

Writing

Write about your idea of a dapper outfit. Use **dapper** in your sentences.

_____

_____

_____

curtail

verb

to cut short; reduce

synonym: shorten

Jeff's teacher suggested he **curtail** the time he spends playing video games if he wants to do better on his homework.

Which activities might you **curtail** if you wanted to improve your schoolwork?

- watching television at night
- paying attention in class
- staying up late on school nights
- doing homework
- reading books

List some activities people should **curtail** if they want to stay healthy.

dejected

adjective

low in spirits

synonym: discouraged

Hiroshi felt **dejected** when he didn't break the record for the long jump.

Which words mean about the same as **dejected**?

- lighthearted
- depressed
- elated
- downhearted
- blue

If someone is feeling **dejected**, we might say he or she is "down in the mouth." How might that expression have come to be?

digress

verb

to get off the subject, especially when speaking or writing

The teacher took a moment to **digress** to tell a funny story before getting back to the lesson.

Which of these do you do when you **digress**?

- focus
- lose track
- concentrate
- wander
- get distracted

Why might it be important not to **digress** when you are working in a group to complete an assignment? Can it ever be valuable to **digress**?

heirloom

noun

a valued object handed down from generation to generation

Alana's gold locket was a family **heirloom** that had belonged to her great-grandmother.

Complete the graphic organizer for **heirloom**.

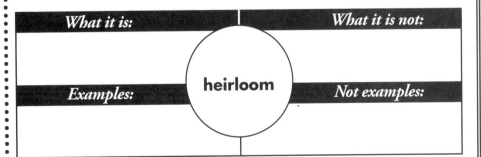

What it is:		*What it is not:*
	heirloom	
Examples:		*Not examples:*

Tell about any **heirlooms** that have been passed down for generations in your family. Do you own something that you might like to pass on as an **heirloom**?

Review

curtail • dejected • digress • heirloom

Write on the board the four words studied this week. Read the words with the class and briefly review their meanings. Then conduct the oral activities below.

1 Tell students that you are going to give them a clue about one of the words for the week. They are to find the word that answers the clue.

- You'd feel this way if your best friend moved away. (**dejected**)

- People do this when they don't stick to the subject. (**digress**)

- A beautiful old piece of furniture might be one. (**an heirloom**)

- You do this when you cut short a discussion. (**curtail it**)

2 Read each sentence and ask students to supply the correct word to complete the sentence.

- After Mom scolded her, our puppy looked ____. (**dejected**)

- Please don't ____. We need to stay on task to get the job done. (**digress**)

- If I ____ my TV watching a bit, I'll have more time for soccer practice. (**curtail**)

- Mom's pearl necklace is an ____ that once belonged to her great-aunt. (**heirloom**)

3 Read each sentence and ask students to tell which word or words are wrong. Then have them provide the correct word from the week's list.

- Let's expand pollution so we can have a cleaner planet. (**expand/curtail**)

- Don't stick to the topic or we'll never finish our discussion. (**stick to the topic/digress**)

- Ana looked so lighthearted that I asked her what was troubling her. (**lighthearted/dejected**)

4 Read each sentence and ask students to decide if it is true or false. If the sentence is false, instruct students to explain why.

- Few heirlooms are brand-new. (**true**)

- Winning contests makes most people feel dejected. (**false; it makes most people feel elated**)

- People can lose weight by curtailing the amount of fat and sugar in their diets. (**true**)

- When you digress, you write about one topic. (**false; you wander from one topic to another**)

Answers for page 87: 1. B, 2. G, 3. D, 4. J

Review Words   curtail • dejected • digress • heirloom

Fill in the bubble next to the correct answer.

1. **Which word is a synonym for *dejected*?**
   - Ⓐ furious
   - Ⓑ discouraged
   - Ⓒ overjoyed
   - Ⓓ interested

2. **Which word is an antonym for *curtail*?**
   - Ⓕ miss
   - Ⓖ extend
   - Ⓗ shorten
   - Ⓙ enjoy

3. **Which phrase means the opposite of *digress*?**
   - Ⓐ stray from the topic
   - Ⓑ go into great detail
   - Ⓒ expand the discussion
   - Ⓓ stick to the subject

4. **Which of these might be a family *heirloom*?**
   - Ⓕ your family's five-year-old dog
   - Ⓖ your little brother's newest toy
   - Ⓗ your mom's new coffeemaker
   - Ⓙ your great-grandma's dining table

Writing ....

Write about a time when you felt dejected. What cheered you up?
Use **dejected** in your sentences.

_____

_____

_____

gregarious

adjective

fond of being with others

synonym: sociable

Because Heather is so **gregarious**, she always has friends around her.

Which of these words would describe a **gregarious** person?

- moody
- friendly
- likeable
- pleasant
- mean

Do you consider yourself to be **gregarious**? Why or why not?

docile

adjective

easy to handle or train

Anita's **docile** dog won the prize for "best-behaved pet" at the show.

Complete the graphic organizer for **docile**.

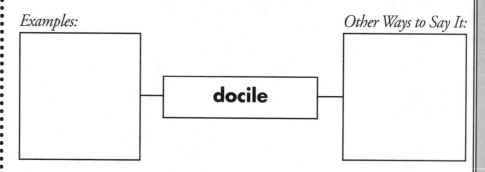

Examples: *Other Ways to Say It:*

docile

What type of behavior do you think Anita's **docile** dog exhibited to be named "best-behaved pet"? Do you prefer **docile** or unmanageable pets?

dexterity

noun

skill in using the hands

After playing the piano for years, Mei-Ling has wonderful **dexterity**.

Which of the following activities require **dexterity**?

- long-distance running
- playing guitar
- knitting
- biking
- stringing beads

Tell about something you do that requires **dexterity**.

fickle

adjective

always changing in interests or loyalty

We weren't surprised when Lisa switched teams at the last minute, because she is often **fickle**.

Which words mean about the same thing as **fickle**?

- flighty
- unpredictable
- definite
- changeable
- stable

Describe a time when you or someone you know acted **fickle**.

gregarious • docile • dexterity • fickle

Write on the board the four words studied this week. Read the words with the class and briefly review their meanings. Then conduct the oral activities below.

1 Tell students that you are going to give them a clue about one of the words for the week. They are to find the word that answers the clue.

- This word describes a gentle, well-trained horse. (**docile**)

- You need this to make jewelry or repair a bike. (**dexterity**)

- This word would describe someone who loves to talk with people. (**gregarious**)

- You could use this word to describe someone whose interests keep changing. (**fickle**)

2 Read each sentence and ask students to supply the correct word to complete the sentence.

- It takes ____ and good eyesight to thread a needle. (**dexterity**)

- Our puppy hasn't been easy to train, but she may grow more ____ as she gets older. (**docile**)

- Even ____ people sometimes enjoy spending time alone. (**gregarious**)

- Alex has always been loyal to me, so I'm surprised to hear you call him ____. (**fickle**)

3 Read each sentence and ask students to tell which word or words are wrong. Then have them provide the correct word from the week's list.

- You can't count on a loyal friend. (**loyal/fickle**)

- I'm a loner—I love to socialize. (**a loner/gregarious**)

- This sweet, unmanageable dog instantly obeys my commands. (**unmanageable/docile**)

- It takes clumsiness to be a good painter. (**clumsiness/dexterity**)

4 Read each sentence and ask students to decide if it is true or false. If the sentence is false, instruct students to explain why.

- Good handwriting requires dexterity. (**true**)

- Gregarious people feel happy in large groups of friends. (**true**)

- *Docile* and *disobedient* are antonyms. (**true**)

- *Fickle* and *loyal* are synonyms. (**false; they are antonyms**)

Answers for page 91: 1. D, 2. G, 3. D, 4. F

Review Words   gregarious • docile • dexterity • fickle

Fill in the bubble next to the correct answer.

1. **Which word is a synonym for *docile*?**
   - Ⓐ sleepy
   - Ⓑ shiny
   - Ⓒ soft
   - Ⓓ gentle

2. **Which word is an antonym for *dexterity*?**
   - Ⓕ childishness
   - Ⓖ clumsiness
   - Ⓗ irritability
   - Ⓙ stinginess

3. **Which word is an antonym for *fickle*?**
   - Ⓐ sensible
   - Ⓑ cheerful
   - Ⓒ handsome
   - Ⓓ consistent

4. **Which activity would a *gregarious* person be most likely to enjoy?**
   - Ⓕ going to a party
   - Ⓖ reading a book
   - Ⓗ taking a walk alone
   - Ⓙ painting a picture

Writing

Write about the most gregarious person you know. Use **gregarious** in your sentences.

_____

_____

_____

brawl

noun

a loud fight

synonym: altercation

When the pitcher accidentally hit the batter with a fastball, a **brawl** broke out between the two teams.

Which of these things might you see in a **brawl**?

- punching
- singing
- kicking
- yelling
- laughing

What are other situations in which you might see a **brawl**? What would you do if a **brawl** started near you?

germinate

verb

to begin to grow

synonym: sprout

The spring rains helped the wildflower seeds to **germinate**.

Complete this graphic organizer for **germinate**.

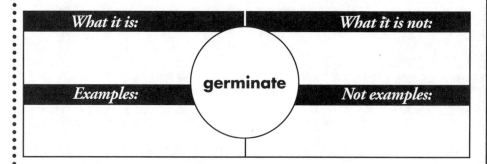

What it is:		*What it is not:*
	germinate	
Examples:		*Not examples:*

What are some of the things you can do to help seeds **germinate**?

classify

verb

to put into groups according to a system

Lilia will **classify** the insects in her collection by color.

Which examples below describe things that have been **classified**?

- Students who ride the school bus lined up first.
- I looked for a book in the fairy tale section of the library.
- This dresser drawer contains T-shirts, socks, and mittens.
- In my reading book there are stories about space travel, how to make your own jewelry, Native American legends, and other topics.
- The chemist stored each type of chemical in its own box.

Name some foods that you could **classify** into these categories: nuts, grains, and legumes.

tedious

adjective

boring; tiresome

Three hours of weeding a garden can be **tedious**.

How might you feel when you are doing something **tedious**?

- jolly
- tired
- excited
- weary
- energetic

What is something **tedious** that you have to do at home?

brawl • germinate • classify • tedious

Write on the board the four words studied this week. Read the words with the class and briefly review their meanings. Then conduct the oral activities below.

1 Tell students that you are going to give them a clue about one of the words for the week. They are to find the word that answers the clue.

- Seeds do this when they begin to grow. **(germinate)**

- You could use this word to describe a boring chore. **(tedious)**

- You do this when you say that a carrot is a vegetable and an orange is a fruit. **(classify them)**

- This is loud and violent. **(a brawl)**

2 Read each sentence and ask students to supply the correct word to complete the sentence.

- Seeds usually ____ in spring. **(germinate)**

- Did you know that scientists ____ tomatoes as fruits? **(classify)**

- I can't wait to finish this ____ chore so I can do something more interesting. **(tedious)**

- Let's settle this argument before it turns into a ____. **(brawl)**

3 Read each list of words and phrases. Ask students to supply the word that fits best with each.

- boring, tiresome, wearisome **(tedious)**

- seeds, sprout, begin to grow **(germinate)**

- shouting, punching, fighting **(brawl)**

- organize, categorize, put into groups **(classify)**

4 Read each sentence and ask students to decide if it is true or false. If the sentence is false, instruct students to explain why.

- Opening birthday presents is a tedious task. **(false; it's exciting rather than boring)**

- Scientists classify dogs as mammals. **(true)**

- Seeds need water to germinate. **(true)**

- Having a brawl is a peaceful way to settle a disagreement. **(false; brawls are angry fights)**

Answers for page 95: 1. B, 2. J, 3. A, 4. G

Name _____

Review Words brawl • germinate • classify • tedious

Fill in the bubble next to the correct answer.

1. **Which word is a synonym for *germinate*?**
   Ⓐ droop
   Ⓑ sprout
   Ⓒ transplant
   Ⓓ trim

2. **Which word is an antonym for *tedious*?**
   Ⓕ clear
   Ⓖ graceful
   Ⓗ familiar
   Ⓙ fascinating

3. **How would you *classify* strawberries?**
   Ⓐ by grouping them with other berries
   Ⓑ by planting, watering, and weeding them
   Ⓒ by picking them
   Ⓓ by eating them

4. **Why might some people get into a *brawl*?**
   Ⓕ to celebrate a special occasion
   Ⓖ because they are angry at one another
   Ⓗ because they have business to discuss
   Ⓙ to travel from one place to another

Writing

Write about the most tedious task you have had to do recently. Use **tedious** in your sentences.

_____

_____

_____

admonish

verb

to caution or warn

synonym: reprimand

Mrs. Wu had to **admonish** her students about running in the hallway.

Which of these are examples of **admonishing** someone?

- A police officer talks to a driver but does not write a ticket.
- A judge sentences a criminal to a year in prison.
- A mother says that next time, her child will go to the "time out" chair.
- A principal explains what happens to students who race their bikes on the playground.
- A father doesn't pay attention when his children tease each other.

Pretend that you are a parent. Your children have just come inside with mud all over their shoes. What would you say to **admonish** them?

foreign

adjective

1. from another country
2. different; strange

We served lots of **foreign** foods at the international celebration. The hamburgers looked **foreign** alongside all the other exotic foods.

Which meaning of the word **foreign** is being used: "from another country" or "different"?

- His intense interest in video games seems foreign to me.
- My dad bought a computer program to learn a foreign language.
- Greece is one foreign land I'd really like to visit.
- After a month of backpacking, sleeping in a bed seemed foreign.
- A movie from Russia won the best foreign film award.

What are some of your favorite **foreign** foods?

gallery

noun

a room or building where art is shown or sold

Ima was impressed by all the colorful paintings in the **gallery**.

Which of these items might you find displayed in a **gallery**?

- paintings
- envelopes
- sculptures
- photographs
- shovels

If you could see any type of exhibit in a **gallery**, what would you choose to see?

harass

verb

to bother repeatedly

My brother shoots rubber bands at me when he wants to **harass** me.

Complete the graphic organizer for **harass**.

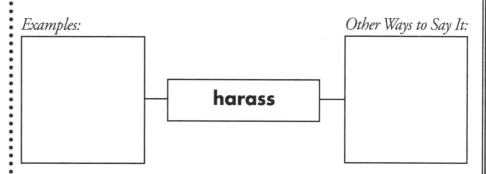

Examples: *Other Ways to Say It:*

harass

What are appropriate ways to respond to someone who is **harassing** you?

admonish • foreign • gallery • harass

Write on the board the four words studied this week. Read the words with the class and briefly review their meanings. Then conduct the oral activities below.

1 Tell students that you are going to give them a clue about one of the words for the week. They are to find the word that answers the clue.

- This word describes another country's customs. **(foreign)**

- Dogs may do this to cats by chasing them repeatedly. **(harass them)**

- Artists show their work to the public in this space. **(a gallery)**

- Dads do this to warn their kids not to cross the street unless it is safe. **(admonish them)**

2 Read each sentence and ask students to supply the correct word to complete the sentence.

- Dad changed the ingredients, so the soup tasted ＿＿ to me. **(foreign)**

- Don't ＿＿ your sister by pulling her hair. **(harass)**

- We visited a ＿＿ to look at Mr. Goldstein's paintings. **(gallery)**

- Police officers may ＿＿ drivers for traffic violations without giving them tickets. **(admonish)**

3 Read each sentence and ask students to tell which word or words are wrong. Then have them provide the correct word from the week's list.

- Mom praised us, warning us not to disobey her again. **(praised/admonished)**

- A school bully made friends with other students by calling them names. **(made friends with/harassed)**

- Sushi, curry, and linguini are considered native foods in the U.S. **(native/foreign)**

4 Read each sentence and ask students to decide if it is true or false. If the sentence is false, instruct students to explain why.

- Galleries display artwork. **(true)**

- *Admonish* and *warn* are synonyms. **(true)**

- A buzzing mosquito might harass you. **(true)**

- *Foreign* and *familiar* are synonyms. **(false; they are antonyms)**

Answers for page 99: 1. C, 2. J, 3. A, 4. G

Review Words   admonish • foreign • gallery • harass

Fill in the bubble next to the correct answer.

1. **Which word is a synonym for *harass*?**
   Ⓐ question
   Ⓑ encourage
   Ⓒ torment
   Ⓓ warn

2. **Which word is an antonym for *foreign*?**
   Ⓕ exotic
   Ⓖ faraway
   Ⓗ different
   Ⓙ familiar

3. **Why might a teacher *admonish* her students?**
   Ⓐ to warn them to study harder for the next vocabulary quiz
   Ⓑ to praise them for the great work they did on art projects
   Ⓒ to encourage them to love reading fiction and poetry
   Ⓓ to thank them for raising money for school sports programs

4. **Which of these would you be most likely to see at a *gallery*?**
   Ⓕ a popular new comedy movie
   Ⓖ drawings and paintings on display
   Ⓗ refrigerators and ovens for sale
   Ⓙ tables filled with hungry customers

Writing

Write about a foreign country that you would like to visit. Tell why you'd like to go there. Use **foreign** in your sentences.

_____

_____

indulge

verb

to allow yourself to enjoy something

Adrianne fought the urge to **indulge** her craving for the rich chocolate dessert.

Which of these situations would describe a person who is **indulging** in something?

- Mother went to the spa for a manicure.
- Ryan knew he had to mow the lawn before it got dark.
- It's my turn to cook, so I have to go to the grocery store.
- Have some popcorn and watch your favorite movie.
- We ordered the most expensive meals on the menu.

What activities do you **indulge** in for pleasure? Can **indulging** ever be bad?

destitute

adjective

having no money or other means of living

The fifth-graders raised money to help **destitute** people in their community.

Which of these words mean about the same as **destitute**?

- penniless
- affluent
- needy
- poverty-stricken
- impoverished

What can communities do to help those who are **destitute**?

jumble

noun

a confused mess

The **jumble** of books in the box made it impossible to find what I was looking for.

Complete the graphic organizer for **jumble**.

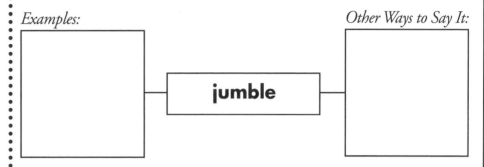

Examples:

jumble

Other Ways to Say It:

Do you like having things in your room in a **jumble**? Why or why not?

lecture

noun

a prepared talk about something

verb

to scold

The park ranger gave a **lecture** about wild animals. He told about having to **lecture** some campers about leaving food out for the bears.

Which meaning of **lecture** is being described: a "prepared talk" or "scolding someone"?

- Mom lectured me when I got ink on the new couch.
- The principal lectured for 10 minutes on the school rules.
- The students gathered in the auditorium to hear a guest speaker give a lecture.
- The coach wagged his finger at the players as he lectured them about the rules.
- The former president is often invited to give lectures at large gatherings.

Tell about the subject of a **lecture** you have attended.

Review

Week 25
A Word a Day

indulge • destitute • jumble • lecture

Write on the board the four words studied this week. Read the words with the class and briefly review their meanings. Then conduct the oral activities below.

1 Tell students that you are going to give them a clue about one of the words for the week. They are to find the word that answers the clue.

- This word describes someone with no money at all. (**destitute**)

- If the items in your closet are in this state, it will be hard to find things quickly. (**a jumble**)

- People do this when they eat delicious foods filled with fat and sugar. (**indulge**)

- A scientist might give one to inform people about rainforest creatures. (**a lecture**)

2 Read each sentence and ask students to supply the correct word to complete the sentence.

- On some weekends, I ____ in watching movies and eating junk food. (**indulge**)

- Don't ____ me about keeping my room tidy. Yours is messier than mine is. (**lecture**)

- How can you find your homework in the ____ of papers on your desk? (**jumble**)

- The charity provided job training to help ____ people have a chance to support themselves. (**destitute**)

3 Read each sentence and ask students to tell which word or words are wrong. Then have them provide the correct word from the week's list.

- This wealthy family has no home and no money for food. (**wealthy/destitute**)

- The kitchen utensil drawer is in such an organized state, I never did find the can opener. (**an organized state/a jumble**)

- If I curtail eating desserts, I will gain weight. (**curtail/indulge in**)

4 Read each sentence and ask students to decide if it is true or false. If the sentence is false, instruct students to explain why.

- Most lectures are meant to be educational. (**true**)

- Destitute people desperately need help. (**true**)

- It is pleasurable to indulge yourself. (**true**)

- *Jumble* and *order* are synonyms. (**false; they are antonyms**)

Answers for page 103: 1. A, 2. F, 3. B, 4. F

| **Review Words** | indulge • destitute • jumble • lecture |

Fill in the bubble next to the correct answer.

1. **Which word is a synonym for *lecture*?**
   - Ⓐ scold
   - Ⓑ praise
   - Ⓒ tease
   - Ⓓ encourage

2. **Which phrase describes a *jumble*?**
   - Ⓕ clothes all over the floor
   - Ⓖ socks sorted by color
   - Ⓗ spices in alphabetical order
   - Ⓙ everything in its place

3. **People *indulge* in certain activities because they are ____.**
   - Ⓐ harmful
   - Ⓑ pleasurable
   - Ⓒ troublesome
   - Ⓓ challenging

4. **Which word is an antonym for *destitute*?**
   - Ⓕ wealthy
   - Ⓖ impoverished
   - Ⓗ educated
   - Ⓙ ignorant

Writing

Write about a food that tastes good but isn't very good for you. Use **indulge** in your sentences.

_____

_____

maneuver

verb

to move carefully and skillfully

Mika tried to **maneuver** his bike around the cones on the obstacle course.

Which of these situations would require skillful **maneuvering**?

- entering a narrow harbor with a cruise ship
- walking to the kitchen to get a snack
- moving through a video game maze
- carrying an armload of packages through a glass shop
- driving on a city street crowded with cars, bikes, and pedestrians

Describe a situation in which you had to **maneuver** carefully.

frantic

adjective

very excited with worry or fear

Lihn was so **frantic** that she'd miss the bus for the field trip that she ran all the way to school.

Complete the graphic organizer for **frantic**.

Examples: **frantic**   *Other Ways to Say It:*

Tell about a time when you were **frantic**. Why were you **frantic**? How did you feel? What did you do?

peer

noun

a person of the same age or ability level

Even though Daisy is Roberto's **peer**, she is three inches taller than he is.

Which of these people would be your **peer**?

- your mother
- students in your class
- your grandfather
- the kids on your baseball team
- your best friend

Name three of your **peers** and three of your parents' **peers**.

stagnant

adjective

not moving or flowing

synonym: still

When a puddle of water is **stagnant**, harmful bacteria can grow in it.

Which of the following could be described as **stagnant**?

- the air in a room that had been closed up for a week
- a waterfall
- a pond with a layer of algae on top
- a filled aquarium tank without plants or fish
- air in a room with a fan turned on

Where might you find **stagnant** water?

maneuver • frantic • peer • stagnant

Write on the board the four words studied this week. Read the words with the class and briefly review their meanings. Then conduct the oral activities below.

1 Tell students that you are going to give them a clue about one of the words for the week. They are to find the word that answers the clue.

- You could use this word to describe water in a broken fountain. **(stagnant)**

- This is someone who is about your age. **(a peer)**

- Drivers do this with cars, and bicyclists do this with bikes. **(maneuver them)**

- A mom might feel this way if her young child got lost in a supermarket. **(frantic)**

2 Read each sentence and ask students to supply the correct word to complete the sentence.

- Don't drink water from a ____ pond. **(stagnant)**

- We were ____ with worry until we found our lost cat. **(frantic)**

- A ____ of my grandpa's, Mr. Ramirez, is 65 years old. **(peer)**

- It can be hard to ____ your bike around cars and pedestrians in parking lots. **(maneuver)**

3 Read each sentence and ask students to tell which word or words are wrong. Then have them provide the correct word from the week's list.

- Jill is an elder of mine. In fact, she is exactly my age. **(an elder/a peer)**

- Mom was calm when she realized that her valuable ring was missing. **(calm/frantic)**

- That birdbath is filled with moving water that has not been replaced in months. **(moving/stagnant)**

4 Read each sentence and ask students to decide if it is true or false. If the sentence is false, instruct students to explain why.

- Stagnant water flows swiftly. **(false; it just sits there)**

- It is hard to calm down when you are frantic. **(true)**

- Your grandparents are your peers. **(false; they are not in your age group)**

- *Maneuver* and *steer* are synonyms. **(true)**

Answers for page 107: 1. C, 2. J, 3. D, 4. F

| **Review Words** | maneuver • frantic • peer • stagnant |

Fill in the bubble next to the correct answer.

1. Which word is a synonym for *frantic*?

Ⓐ elated

Ⓑ irritated

Ⓒ desperate

Ⓓ calm

2. Which phrase means the opposite of *peer*?

Ⓕ someone who knows the same things you know

Ⓖ someone who is in your class at school

Ⓗ someone who was born the same year you were born

Ⓙ someone from a different generation

3. Which is an example of *stagnant* water?

Ⓐ an ocean

Ⓑ a rushing river

Ⓒ a creek that flows downhill

Ⓓ still water in a small pond

4. How does a bicyclist *maneuver* a bike?

Ⓕ by moving the handlebars

Ⓖ by keeping it in good repair

Ⓗ by saving up enough money to buy it

Ⓙ by putting on the brakes and getting off

Writing

Write about a time when you have had to maneuver through a crowd.
Use **maneuver** in your sentences.

_____

_____

_____

unkempt

adjective

not groomed;
not neat or tidy

After a week of camping in the wilderness, everybody looked quite **unkempt**.

Which words mean about the same thing as **unkempt**?

- messy
- orderly
- scruffy
- rumpled
- elegant

Is it ever OK with your parents for you to look **unkempt**? When? When won't they allow it?

humdrum

adjective

lacking variety or excitement

synonym:
monotonous

The movie was so **humdrum** that I fell asleep.

Which of the following describe something that is **humdrum**?

- watching paint dry
- going to a swimming party
- listening to a fly buzz
- going horseback riding
- spending a day at an amusement park

What are some activities that you find **humdrum**?

replenish

verb

to refill

After the long race, the runners had to **replenish** the water in their bodies.

Complete the graphic organizer for **replenish**.

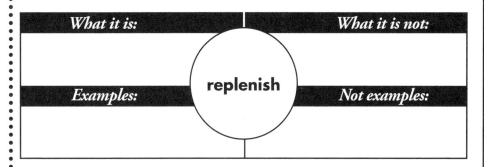

What it is:		*What it is not:*
	replenish	
Examples:		*Not examples:*

What types of foods do you eat to **replenish** your body with nutrients?

agriculture

noun

the science of growing crops and raising livestock

synonym: farming

My uncle studied **agriculture** in college and now grows organic tomatoes that he sells to restaurants.

Which activities would be performed by someone who works in **agriculture**?

- milking cows
- planting seeds
- driving a taxicab
- driving a tractor
- serving food in a restaurant

Name some of the products of **agriculture** that you eat.

Review

unkempt • humdrum • replenish • agriculture

Write on the board the four words studied this week. Read the words with the class and briefly review their meanings. Then conduct the oral activities below.

1 Tell students that you are going to give them a clue about one of the words for the week. They are to find the word that answers the clue.

- This word describes boring household chores. (**humdrum**)

- Farmers work in this business. (**agriculture**)

- Waiters do this when customers empty their water glasses. (**replenish them**)

- You could use this word to describe someone's uncombed hair. (**unkempt**)

2 Read each sentence and ask students to supply the correct word to complete the sentence.

- Mowing the lawn can be a ____ job, but I enjoy it. (**humdrum**)

- Allow me to ____ your glass of juice. (**replenish**)

- Ira's ____ hair showed that he had just awakened. (**unkempt**)

- We can thank the science of ____ for the variety of fruits and vegetables we eat. (**agriculture**)

3 Read each sentence and ask students to tell which word or words are wrong. Then have them provide the correct word from the week's list.

- I've finished all of the water in my glass. Please empty it for me. (**empty/replenish**)

- I looked neat and tidy after playing soccer all day. (**neat and tidy/unkempt**)

- I don't mind doing exciting chores such as clearing the table. (**exciting/humdrum**)

- Mr. Johnson works in the mining business. He raises cattle and grows apples. (**mining/agriculture**)

4 Read each sentence and ask students to decide if it is true or false. If the sentence is false, instruct students to explain why.

- Agriculture provides us with milk and eggs. (**true**)

- Drinking water helps to replenish our bodies' fluids. (**true**)

- Most people look unkempt at weddings. (**false; most people at weddings look well dressed**)

- *Humdrum* and *boring* are synonyms. (**true**)

Answers for page 111: 1. C, 2. G, 3. C, 4. H

Review Words unkempt • humdrum • replenish • agriculture

Fill in the bubble next to the correct answer.

1. **Which word is a synonym for *replenish*?**
   - Ⓐ stir
   - Ⓑ shake
   - Ⓒ restore
   - Ⓓ review

2. **Which word is an antonym for *humdrum*?**
   - Ⓕ slender
   - Ⓖ exciting
   - Ⓗ silent
   - Ⓙ boring

3. **Who works in *agriculture*?**
   - Ⓐ a teacher
   - Ⓑ a lawyer
   - Ⓒ a rancher
   - Ⓓ an actor

4. **Who is likely to have an *unkempt* appearance?**
   - Ⓕ a model on a magazine cover
   - Ⓖ a bride and groom at their wedding
   - Ⓗ someone who just got out of bed
   - Ⓙ someone who just combed his hair

Writing

Write about a humdrum activity. What makes it humdrum? Use **humdrum** in your sentences.

_____

_____

_____

barricade

verb

to block off

noun

a barrier used to block passage

The fire department had to **barricade** the streets for the parade. They parked their firetrucks across the crosswalks to make a **barricade**.

Which of these are situations when **barricades** might be used?

- The new park is now open to the public.
- There is a dangerous hole in the roadway.
- Traffic is diverted due to a fire hydrant breaking.
- Anyone may use this parking lot.
- The crowds weren't allowed to get close to the movie set.

Who might create a **barricade**? What might be used to create a **barricade**?

betray

verb

to not be loyal or faithful to

Kin Yui didn't mean to **betray** Laura's secret when she told Ana. She thought Ana already knew about it.

Which word or words mean about the same as **betray**?

- guard
- double-cross
- protect
- let down
- reveal

We count on our friends to be true to us and not **betray** our trust. What are some examples of how you or someone you know have been **betrayed**?

complement

noun

something that makes something else complete

Cinderella's glass slippers were the perfect **complement** to her gown.

Which of these items are **complements** to each other?

- ice cream and cake
- combat boots and ballet slippers
- burger and fries
- bat and ball
- peanut butter and jelly

Name some food items that you think are great **complements**.

defiant

adjective

bold in standing up against someone or something

The colonists were **defiant** when the king's soldiers ordered them to return home.

Complete the graphic organizer for **defiant**.

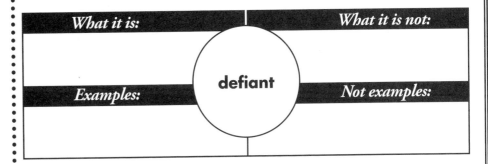

When is it good to be **defiant**? When is it not such a good idea?

barricade • betray • complement • defiant

Write on the board the four words studied this week. Read the words with the class and briefly review their meanings. Then conduct the oral activities below.

1 Tell students that you are going to give them a clue about one of the words for the week. They are to find the word that answers the clue.

- On a sandwich, peanut butter is one for jelly. **(a complement)**

- You could use this word to describe protest marchers. **(defiant)**

- Someone does this when he or she promises to support a person and then fails to do so. **(betrays that person)**

- Workers sometimes do this to roads during construction projects. **(barricade them)**

2 Read each sentence and ask students to supply the correct word to complete the sentence.

- The ____ four-year-old refused to put on her shoes. **(defiant)**

- Please do not ____ my secret to anyone. **(betray)**

- To me, cereal needs milk as its ____. **(complement)**

- Police officers put up a ____ to block the damaged bridge. **(barricade)**

3 Read each list of words and phrases. Ask students to supply the word that fits best with each.

- bold, angry, disobedient, resistant **(defiant)**

- bread and butter, shoes and socks, partners, two halves of a whole **(complements)**

- block off, keep people out, construct a barrier **(barricade)**

- let down, reveal a secret, break an agreement **(betray)**

4 Read each sentence and ask students to decide if it is true or false. If the sentence is false, instruct students to explain why.

- You would feel hurt and angry if a friend betrayed you. **(true)**

- A speed bump is a barricade. **(false; it slows down cars but does not block them off)**

- Standing up to a bully may require defiant behavior. **(true)**

- Blue jeans and T-shirts are complements. **(true)**

Answers for page 115: 1. D, 2. H, 3. C, 4. G

Name _____

Review Words · barricade • betray • complement • defiant

Fill in the bubble next to the correct answer.

1. **Which word is an antonym for *defiant*?**
   - Ⓐ bold
   - Ⓑ certain
   - Ⓒ furious
   - Ⓓ obedient

2. **Which word is a synonym for *barricade*?**
   - Ⓕ highway
   - Ⓖ skyscraper
   - Ⓗ barrier
   - Ⓙ gateway

3. **Which is a *complement* to a slice of toast?**
   - Ⓐ a toaster
   - Ⓑ flour
   - Ⓒ butter
   - Ⓓ a plate

4. **How do people usually feel when others *betray* them?**
   - Ⓕ surprised and happy
   - Ⓖ hurt and angry
   - Ⓗ relieved and thankful
   - Ⓙ mildly amused

Writing

Write about a time when you were defiant. What was the reason?
What happened? Use **defiant** in your sentences.

_____

_____

_____

diligent

adjective

hardworking

Amy is a **diligent** student who always turns in her homework on time.

Which of the following describe a **diligent** worker?

- comes to work early
- takes long lunch breaks
- doesn't care if the job is done on time
- takes lots of long vacations
- works late to get the job done

Describe the study habits of a **diligent** student.

efficient

adjective

doing a job in a timely manner with the least amount of effort or materials

Pete was such an **efficient** busboy that he could stack and carry all the plates on the table at once.

Which words describe someone who is **efficient**?

- slow
- time-saving
- capable
- confused
- effective

What do you think is the most **efficient** way to figure out how many students there are in your grade at school?

outwit

verb

to be more clever than someone else

Edmond always won at chess because he could **outwit** any player he faced.

Which words would describe someone who is able to **outwit** an opponent?

- smart
- slow
- sly
- cunning
- tricky

Give examples of situations in which people try to **outwit** each other.

glamorous

adjective

attractive and exciting

synonym: enchanting

Heads turned as the **glamorous** movie star walked down the red carpet.

Complete the graphic organizer for **glamorous**.

What it is:	What it is not:
Examples:	Not examples:

Describe someone you think is **glamorous**. What makes that person seem that way?

Review

diligent • efficient • outwit • glamorous

Write on the board the four words studied this week. Read the words with the class and briefly review their meanings. Then conduct the oral activities below.

1 Tell students that you are going to give them a clue about one of the words for the week. They are to find the word that answers the clue.

- You need cleverness to do this to someone. (**outwit him or her**)

- You could use this word to describe a pretty woman in fancy clothes. (**glamorous**)

- This word describes someone who works hard. (**diligent**)

- This word describes someone who is so well-organized that he or she can complete jobs easily and quickly. (**efficient**)

2 Read each sentence and ask students to supply the correct word to complete the sentence.

- Dad is so ____ that he can cook dinner in 20 minutes. (**efficient**)

- You can raise your grade from a C to a B if you are ____ about doing your homework. (**diligent**)

- Photographers kept snapping pictures of the ____ stars in fancy gowns. (**glamorous**)

- Pablo has figured out how to ____ his friends at card games. (**outwit**)

3 Read each list of words and phrases. Ask students to supply the word that fits best with each.

- charming, elegant, beautifully dressed, fancy (**glamorous**)

- hardworking, dedicated, responsible (**diligent**)

- strategize, outthink, cleverly defeat, trick (**outwit**)

- well-organized, capable, quick, effective (**efficient**)

4 Read each sentence and ask students to decide if it is true or false. If the sentence is false, instruct students to explain why.

- A fashion model might look glamorous even in blue jeans. (**true**)

- When you play a game with someone and outwit him or her, you are the loser. (**false; you use cleverness to win**)

- An efficient person works quickly and well. (**true**)

- A diligent worker is lazy. (**false; he or she is hardworking**)

Answers for page 119: 1. D, 2. H, 3. D, 4. H

Name _____

Fill in the bubble next to the correct answer.

1. **Which word is a synonym for *efficient*?**
   Ⓐ cautious
   Ⓑ conceited
   Ⓒ sloppy
   Ⓓ effective

2. **Which word is an antonym for *diligent*?**
   Ⓕ clever
   Ⓖ hardworking
   Ⓗ lazy
   Ⓙ ignorant

3. **Where would you be most likely to see *glamorous* people?**
   Ⓐ at the supermarket
   Ⓑ at an elementary school
   Ⓒ on a farm or cattle ranch
   Ⓓ at a fancy restaurant

4. **What does a person need to *outwit* someone else?**
   Ⓕ strength
   Ⓖ kindness
   Ⓗ cleverness
   Ⓙ beauty

Writing

Write about a job or chore that you can do efficiently. Use **efficient** in your sentences.

_____

_____

_____

hazardous

adjective

dangerous

antonym: safe

A curvy road becomes even more **hazardous** during heavy rainstorms.

Complete the graphic organizer for **hazardous**.

Examples:

Other Ways to Say It:

hazardous

Describe a **hazardous** situation you have seen or know about.

ventriloquist

noun

an entertainer who speaks without moving his or her lips

The **ventriloquist** made it look like his wooden dummy was telling the jokes.

Which words describe a **ventriloquist**?

- talented
- creative
- uninteresting
- entertaining
- unskilled

Try to act like a **ventriloquist**.

ingenious

adjective

clever or skillful,
especially at inventing
or solving problems

The **ingenious** children made a skateboard
using old roller skates and a piece of wood.

Which words mean about the same thing as **ingenious**?

- dimwitted
- bright
- inventive
- slow
- able

Share some examples of **ingenious** ideas that you or
someone else have had.

knickknack

noun

a small ornament or
decorative object

synonym: trinket

The souvenir shop at the amusement park was
full of **knickknacks**.

Which of the following items are **knickknacks**?

- handmade mittens
- a small porcelain dog
- a fishing rod
- a glass egg
- a ceramic cow

Do you have a **knickknack** that is special to you? Tell the
class about it. Are there any **knickknacks** that you like to
collect?

Review

hazardous • ventriloquist • ingenious • knickknack

Write on the board the four words studied this week. Read the words with the class and briefly review their meanings. Then conduct the oral activities below.

1 Tell students that you are going to give them a clue about one of the words for the week. They are to find the word that answers the clue.

- This kind of entertainer usually uses a dummy. (**a ventriloquist**)

- You probably have at least one on your shelves. (**a knickknack**)

- This word describes harmful chemicals. (**hazardous**)

- This word describes clever, creative solutions to problems. (**ingenious**)

2 Read each sentence and ask students to supply the correct word to complete the sentence.

- Danny's favorite ____ is a china dolphin that his mom gave him. (**knickknack**)

- The ____ has a dummy that looks just like him, except that it is smaller. (**ventriloquist**)

- A sign on the truck says: "Danger: This vehicle carries ____ materials." (**hazardous**)

- An inventor's job is to figure out ____ solutions to everyday problems. (**ingenious**)

3 Read each list of words and phrases. Ask students to supply the word that fits best with each.

- trinket, ornament, souvenir, figurine (**knickknack**)

- dangerous, perilous, unsafe, harmful (**hazardous**)

- entertainer with a dummy on his lap, speaks without lip movement (**ventriloquist**)

- creative, clever, skillful, brilliant, inventive (**ingenious**)

4 Read each sentence and ask students to decide if it is true or false. If the sentence is false, instruct students to explain why.

- Ingenious people invented computers. (**true**)

- Most knickknacks are larger than a basketball. (**false; most knickknacks are much smaller**)

- A ventriloquist speaks without appearing to speak. (**true**)

- Milk is a hazardous liquid. (**false; milk isn't dangerous**)

Answers for page 123: 1. A, 2. G, 3. D, 4. G

Review Words   hazardous • ventriloquist • ingenious • knickknack

Fill in the bubble next to the correct answer.

1. **Which word is a synonym for _ingenious_?**
   - Ⓐ clever
   - Ⓑ clumsy
   - Ⓒ careful
   - Ⓓ daring

2. **Which word is an antonym for _hazardous_?**
   - Ⓕ empty
   - Ⓖ safe
   - Ⓗ tidy
   - Ⓙ clean

3. **Where would you be most likely to see _knickknacks_?**
   - Ⓐ on a towel rack in someone's bathroom
   - Ⓑ on the ceiling of someone's bedroom
   - Ⓒ in a drawer in someone's kitchen
   - Ⓓ on a shelf in someone's living room

4. **A _ventriloquist_ entertains people by doing what?**
   - Ⓕ ice-skating
   - Ⓖ speaking
   - Ⓗ dancing
   - Ⓙ performing magic

Writing

Write a description of a knickknack that you like. Use **knickknack** in your sentences.

_____

_____

_____

landscape

verb

to make the natural features of an outdoor area more attractive by adding trees or plants

noun

an area of land that you can view from one place

After we **landscape** the yard, the **landscape** outside the living room window will be more pleasant.

If you helped to **landscape** a yard, which of these tasks might you do?

- paint a picture
- dig a hole
- buy some flowering plants
- scatter fertilizer on the soil
- sit in a swing

What is your favorite type of **landscape**? Do you like the mountains, the desert, or the beach?

lenient

adjective

not strict in enforcing rules and restrictions

synonym: permissive

Mrs. Johnson was so **lenient** about deadlines that most students turned in their projects late with no consequence.

Complete the graphic organizer for **lenient**.

Examples: *Other Ways to Say It:*

```
┌──────────┐                    ┌──────────┐
│          │        ┌────────┐  │          │
│          │────────│ lenient│──│          │
│          │        └────────┘  │          │
└──────────┘                    └──────────┘
```

Describe someone you know who is **lenient**.

kowtow

verb

1. to show respect or unquestioning obedience
2. in traditional China, to bow from a kneeling position where the forehead touches the ground as a way to show respect

Although I am not required to get on the ground and **kowtow** to my parents, I am expected to **kowtow** to their wishes by never talking back to them.

Which of these people would children **kowtow** to in ancient China?

- a baby
- their grandfather
- a teacher
- the emperor
- their classmates

Have you ever felt like someone expects you to **kowtow** to him or her? How did you feel about it?

justify

verb

to give a good reason or cause for something

Mark knew he could **justify** getting home from school late by explaining that the bus got a flat tire.

Which of these situations could you probably **justify**?

- swatting a fly
- stealing a diamond ring
- returning a library book after the due date
- eating a piece of your sister's Halloween candy
- lying to your teacher

Tell about a time when you avoided getting in trouble because you could **justify** your behavior.

landscape • lenient • kowtow • justify

Write on the board the four words studied this week. Read the words with the class and briefly review their meanings. Then conduct the oral activities below.

1 Tell students that you are going to give them a clue about one of the words for the week. They are to find the word that answers the clue.

- When you do this, you give reasons for something you did. **(justify it)**

- If you look out at the land or ocean from a viewpoint, this is what you see. **(a landscape)**

- In ancient China, people did this to show respect and obedience to others. **(kowtowed)**

- This word describes someone who isn't strict. **(lenient)**

2 Read each sentence and ask students to supply the correct word to complete the sentence.

- I'm not going to ____ to Emma. She's our class president, not our queen. **(kowtow)**

- Mom hired Mr. Jones to ____ our yard. He put in some beautiful new plants. **(landscape)**

- Some students try to ____ tardiness with flimsy excuses. **(justify)**

- Dad is ____ about some rules, but he's strict about bedtime and homework. **(lenient)**

3 Read each list of words and phrases. Ask students to supply the word that fits best with each.

- trees, mountains, fields, lakes, scenery **(landscape)**

- show respect, kneel, bow, pledge obedience **(kowtow)**

- explain, excuse, provide reasons for your actions **(justify)**

- willing to bend the rules, lax about enforcing laws **(lenient)**

4 Read each sentence and ask students to decide if it is true or false. If the sentence is false, instruct students to explain why.

- A parking lot is a landscape. **(false; a parking lot isn't a natural outdoor space)**

- A lenient teacher expects her students to follow every rule. **(false; a lenient teacher is not strict)**

- Some workers kowtow to their bosses. **(true)**

- Justifying an action doesn't necessarily make it OK. **(true)**

Answers for page 127: 1. B, 2. F, 3. B, 4. H

Review Words   landscape • lenient • kowtow • justify

Fill in the bubble next to the correct answer.

1. **Which word is a synonym for _kowtow_?**
   Ⓐ stand
   Ⓑ bow
   Ⓒ sit
   Ⓓ twirl

2. **Which word is an antonym for _lenient_?**
   Ⓕ strict
   Ⓖ unfair
   Ⓗ welcoming
   Ⓙ irritable

3. **How do people _landscape_ their yards?**
   Ⓐ by adding outdoor furniture
   Ⓑ by adding trees and other plants
   Ⓒ by building new swimming pools
   Ⓓ by paving their yards with concrete

4. **Which word or phrase could be used instead of _justify_ in this sentence?**
   How can you justify the fact that you took your sister's sweater without asking?
   Ⓕ deny
   Ⓖ laugh about
   Ⓗ reasonably explain
   Ⓙ sincerely apologize for

Writing

Should parents be strict or lenient with their kids about bedtimes?
Write your opinion. Use **lenient** in your sentences.

_____

_____

enthusiasm

noun

a strong feeling of excitement or interest

synonym: eagerness

Stella's **enthusiasm** for the ballet soon had the whole class eager to attend the performance.

Complete the graphic organizer for **enthusiasm**.

Examples: | **enthusiasm** | *Other Ways to Say It:*

What makes you feel **enthusiasm**? How do you express it?

establish

verb

to set up

The telephone company decided to first **establish** Internet service in large cities before setting it up in small towns.

Which of these do you do when you **establish** something?

- form something new
- demolish something
- install something new
- create something
- eliminate something

When was the United States of America **established** as an independent nation?

flounder

noun

a flatfish that lives in saltwater

verb

to struggle through something, either physically or mentally

After **floundering** through the deep, wet sand at the sea's edge, imagine my surprise at finding a **flounder** in the cuff of my pants.

Which of these might **flounder**?

- a cat that falls into a tub full of water
- a runner headed for the finish line
- someone trying to learn a complicated computer program
- a ballerina performing onstage
- a student whose science project isn't working out

Have you ever **floundered** when trying to learn something new? What was it? How did things turn out?

frigid

adjective

extremely cold

There is no swimming in this mountain lake, as the water in it remains **frigid** even in the summer.

Which of these would be **frigid**?

- a January morning in New York
- the summit of Mount Everest
- a sand castle
- an iceberg
- a July afternoon in Florida

Have you ever been swimming in **frigid** water? Have you ever been outdoors in **frigid** weather? Tell your class about it.

enthusiasm • establish • flounder • frigid

Write on the board the four words studied this week. Read the words with the class and briefly review their meanings. Then conduct the oral activities below.

1 Tell students that you are going to give them a clue about one of the words for the week. They are to find the word that answers the clue.

- This word describes the North Pole's weather. **(frigid)**

- Business people do this when they start new companies. **(establish them)**

- One meaning of this word is a kind of flatfish. **(flounder)**

- This is what you probably feel when you're looking forward to an exciting event. **(enthusiasm)**

2 Read each sentence and ask students to supply the correct word to complete the sentence.

- The weather is _____ today, so please wear your warmest clothes. **(frigid)**

- Knee-deep in snow, we had to _____ across the field to reach our car. **(flounder)**

- My cousin plans to _____ a computer software company after he graduates from college. **(establish)**

- The kids showed their _____ by jumping up and down and cheering loudly. **(enthusiasm)**

3 Read each list of words and phrases. Ask students to supply the word that fits best with each.

- tuna, salmon, bass, halibut **(flounder)**

- cold, freezing, icy, snowy, wintry **(frigid)**

- interest, excitement, eagerness **(enthusiasm)**

- set up a business, start a new university, begin a fashion trend **(establish)**

4 Read each sentence and ask students to decide if it is true or false. If the sentence is false, instruct students to explain why.

- The Founding Fathers established the United States in the 1700s. **(true)**

- Polar bears live in a frigid climate. **(true)**

- If math is easy for you, you are likely to flounder with the assignments. **(false; you flounder when something is difficult)**

- *Enthusiasm* and *boredom* are antonyms. **(true)**

Answers for page 131: 1. D, 2. F, 3. C, 4. H

Review Words   enthusiasm • establish • flounder • frigid

Fill in the bubble next to the correct answer.

1. **Which word is an antonym for *frigid*?**
   - Ⓐ stormy
   - Ⓑ frozen
   - Ⓒ cool
   - Ⓓ boiling

2. **Which word is a synonym for *enthusiasm*?**
   - Ⓕ excitement
   - Ⓖ exhaustion
   - Ⓗ ferocity
   - Ⓙ calmness

3. **In which sentence is the word *flounder* used correctly?**
   - Ⓐ The recipe says to flounder the fish before frying it in oil.
   - Ⓑ Did you look for your jacket in the lost and flounder?
   - Ⓒ The explorers had to flounder through the swamp to reach the camp.
   - Ⓓ In which country can the city of Madrid be flounder?

4. **Which word or phrase could be used instead of *establish* in this sentence?**
   In what year did your grandfather establish his candy manufacturing company?
   - Ⓕ sell
   - Ⓖ buy
   - Ⓗ set up
   - Ⓙ close down

Writing

Write about a kind of business that you would like to establish. Use **establish** in your sentences.

_____

_____

_____

narrative

noun

a story or narration

Ms. Sanchez read the class a first-person **narrative** written by a soldier in the Civil War.

Complete the graphic organizer for **narrative**.

Examples:

narrative

Other Ways to Say It:

What is a **narrative** that you have enjoyed reading or listening to?

patriot

noun

someone who loves and supports his or her country

During the American Revolution, many **patriots** fought against the British for the independence of the colonies.

Which of these people would you describe as a **patriot**? Why?

- a person who works for fair laws
- a person who votes in every election
- a person who complains about government, but does not vote
- a person who stands when the flag passes by in a parade
- a person who spies on his country for another country

Describe some of the ways that you can show you are a **patriot**.

perennial

adjective

lasting for a long time; never ending

noun

a plant that blooms or grows for many years without needing to be replanted

If you have a **perennial** dislike for buying new plants every year, plant some **perennials** in your garden.

Which of these could be considered **perennial** or a **perennial**?

- Feelings of love for your family
- The first day of school
- A 50-year-old oak tree
- Oats that a farmer plants every autumn
- Children not wanting to clean their rooms

Which books or TV shows are your **perennial** favorites? Which ones have you lost interest in?

penetrate

verb

to go into or pass through something

The attackers could not **penetrate** the stone walls of the castle.

Which of these describe something being **penetrated**?

- plant thorns can't stick in the hide of a rhinoceros
- a tetanus shot is needed if you step on a nail
- explorers used machetes to move through the thick jungle
- liquids bounce off the water-resistant fabric
- the dart stuck in the dartboard

What would you do if you had to **penetrate** very hard soil in order to make a hole to plant a tree?

---

narrative • patriot • perennial • penetrate

Write on the board the four words studied this week. Read the words with the class and briefly review their meanings. Then conduct the oral activities below.

1 Tell students that you are going to give them a clue about one of the words for the week. They are to find the word that answers the clue.

- This person wants to serve his or her country. **(a patriot)**

- If you stepped on a tack, it might do this to the sole of your shoe. **(penetrate it)**

- Storytellers tell these. **(narratives)**

- This kind of plant can grow for many years after it is planted. **(a perennial)**

2 Read each sentence and ask students to supply the correct word to complete the sentence.

- Natural disasters have been a _____ problem throughout history. **(perennial)**

- It is the duty of a _____ to vote to choose the country's leaders. **(patriot)**

- My sister related a long _____ about an argument she had with her friend. **(narrative)**

- The ground is so hard and dry that it is hard to _____ with a shovel. **(penetrate)**

3 Read each list of words and phrases. Ask students to supply the word that fits best with each.

- break through, dig into, puncture **(penetrate)**

- story, tale, report **(narrative)**

- loves his country, serves her fellow citizens **(patriot)**

- always, constant, enduring **(perennial)**

4 Read each sentence and ask students to decide if it is true or false. If the sentence is false, instruct students to explain why.

- A patriot is someone who betrays her country. **(false; she loves and supports her country)**

- If someone is your perennial enemy, you'll probably never change your opinion about the person. **(true)**

- Termites can penetrate brick walls. **(false; they can eat through wooden walls, though)**

- Fairy tales and folk tales are narratives. **(true)**

Answers for page 135: 1. A, 2. J, 3. B, 4. H

Review Words   narrative • patriot • perennial • penetrate

Fill in the bubble next to the correct answer.

1. **Which word is an antonym for *perennial*?**
   - Ⓐ brief
   - Ⓑ floral
   - Ⓒ endless
   - Ⓓ commercial

2. **Which word is a synonym for *penetrate*?**
   - Ⓕ pave
   - Ⓖ carve
   - Ⓗ separate
   - Ⓙ puncture

3. **Which word is a synonym for *narrative*?**
   - Ⓐ word
   - Ⓑ story
   - Ⓒ book
   - Ⓓ page

4. **Which phrase could be used instead of *patriot* in this sentence?**
   Only a patriot would want to serve as U.S. president. It is a terribly hard job.
   - Ⓕ diligent, efficient worker
   - Ⓖ brilliant college professor
   - Ⓗ person who loves his or her country
   - Ⓙ person who wants to help his or her neighbors

Writing

Write about someone who is a patriot. Use **patriot** in your sentences.

_____

_____

_____

detest

verb

to hate or
strongly dislike

I don't like most vegetables, but what I really **detest** is cabbage.

Which of these words mean about the same as **detest**?

- adore
- despise
- admire
- be disgusted by
- can't stand

Give an example of something that you **detest**.

scavenger

noun

an animal that eats
already dead and
decaying animals

The deer's carcass was soon picked clean by vultures and other **scavengers**.

Which of these statements describe a **scavenger**?

- The pack of hyenas drove the lioness away from her kill.
- My cat caught a mouse in the barn.
- Vultures are circling the meadow in search of a dead animal.
- Rats live in the sewers and feed on garbage they find there.
- A wild rabbit nibbled on the leaves of my lemon tree.

Why are **scavengers** an important part of a food web?

trivial

adjective

of little or no importance

My tiny scratch seemed **trivial** next to Drew's broken arm.

Complete the graphic organizer for **trivial**.

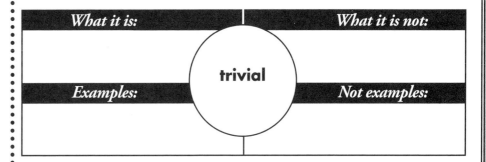

What types of **trivial** matters have you argued about with your friends? Were the arguments worth it?

hemisphere

noun

one half of the Earth; there are four hemispheres: northern and southern; eastern and western

If you live in North America, you live in the northern and western **hemispheres**.

In which **hemispheres** is each of these places located?

- Japan
- Antarctica
- South America
- the United States
- Italy

If you could choose to live anywhere on Earth, which **hemisphere** would you choose?

detest • scavenger • trivial • hemisphere

Write on the board the four words studied this week. Read the words with the class and briefly review their meanings. Then conduct the oral activities below.

1 Tell students that you are going to give them a clue about one of the words for the week. They are to find the word that answers the clue.

- Canada is in the northern one. **(hemisphere)**

- You feel this way when you really don't like something. **(you detest it)**

- This word describes a detail that isn't important. **(trivial)**

- This kind of creature eats animals that predators have already killed. **(a scavenger)**

2 Read each sentence and ask students to supply the correct word to complete the sentence.

- China is in the Earth's eastern _____. **(hemisphere)**

- Let's discuss the most important parts of the book, not the _____ details. **(trivial)**

- Ms. Stanley _____ cheating and deals harshly with any student who does it. **(detests)**

- In addition to killing its own prey, the hyena is an African _____ that eats lions' leftovers. **(scavenger)**

3 Read each list of words and phrases. Ask students to supply the word that fits best with each.

- silly, unimportant, not worth bothering about **(trivial)**

- one half of the globe, northern, southern, eastern, western **(hemisphere)**

- decaying flesh, vulture, ants, carrion-eater **(scavenger)**

- hate, disgusted, can't stand **(detest)**

4 Read each sentence and ask students to decide if it is true or false. If the sentence is false, instruct students to explain why.

- A scavenger kills other animals and eats them. **(false; it eats animals that are already dead)**

- Antarctica is in the southern hemisphere. **(true)**

- Most people detest the smell of garbage. **(true)**

- *Trivial* and *silly* are antonyms. **(false; they are synonyms)**

Answers for page 139: 1. B, 2. J, 3. D, 4. J

Name _____

detest • scavenger • trivial • hemisphere

Fill in the bubble next to the correct answer.

1. **In which two *hemispheres* is the United States located?**
   - Ⓐ the southern and western ones
   - Ⓑ the northern and western ones
   - Ⓒ the southern and eastern ones
   - Ⓓ the northern and eastern ones

2. **Which word is an antonym for *detest*?**
   - Ⓕ dislike
   - Ⓖ measure
   - Ⓗ reject
   - Ⓙ love

3. **Which word is an antonym for *trivial*?**
   - Ⓐ detailed
   - Ⓑ unimportant
   - Ⓒ silly
   - Ⓓ vital

4. **Which word or phrase could be used instead of *scavengers* in this sentence?**
   Scavengers such as vultures benefit from big cats' hunting skills.
   - Ⓕ Vegetarians
   - Ⓖ Predators
   - Ⓗ Creatures that live in large herds or flocks
   - Ⓙ Creatures that eat dead, decaying bodies

Writing

Write about something that is important to you, even though it may seem trivial to others. Use **trivial** in your sentences.

_____

_____

_____

ambition

noun

a strong desire to achieve a specific goal

Mark's **ambition** was to learn to surf.

Complete the graphic organizer for **ambition**.

Examples: **ambition**   *Other Ways to Say It:*

What do you have the **ambition** to learn or do?

dingy

adjective

having a dirty or dull appearance

After years of hanging in the dusty windows, the white lace curtains looked **dingy**.

Which words mean about the same thing as **dingy**?

- bright
- drab
- clean
- soiled
- discolored

What is something in our classroom or school that looks **dingy**?

transmit

verb

1. to pass on from one person or place to another
2. to send out signals by radio or television

When the flu season begins, people try not to **transmit** their germs. Some radio stations even **transmit** information on how to stay healthy.

Which of the following activities could **transmit** germs?

- shouting across the room
- sneezing
- playing kickball
- shaking hands
- drinking from the same cup

How many ways can you think of to **transmit** a message?

encounter

noun

an unexpected meeting

An **encounter** with a bear was the biggest surprise of our hike.

Which of the following describe an **encounter**?

- Two friends meet at a restaurant for lunch.
- You run into a classmate at the park after school.
- You meet a distant cousin at a family reunion.
- Two strangers bump into each other on the street.
- A group of hikers find a rattlesnake coiled next to the path.

Tell about an **encounter** you had with a classmate outside of school.

ambition • dingy • transmit • encounter

Write on the board the four words studied this week. Read the words with the class and briefly review their meanings. Then conduct the oral activities below.

1 Tell students that you are going to give them a clue about one of the words for the week. They are to find the word that answers the clue.

- This word might describe a white T-shirt that someone has worn for a whole week. **(dingy)**

- You would have one of these with someone if you ran into him or her in a supermarket. **(an encounter)**

- People do this when they pass their germs to one another. **(transmit them)**

- People with plenty of this have a good chance of achieving their goals. **(ambition)**

2 Read each sentence and ask students to supply the correct word to complete the sentence.

- An ____ with a rattlesnake can be extremely scary. **(encounter)**

- Pilots use radios to ____ weather information and other messages. **(transmit)**

- Mom's ____ is to own a small clothing store. **(ambition)**

- Please put those ____ clothes in the laundry hamper. **(dingy)**

3 Read each list of words and phrases. Ask students to supply the word that fits best with each.

- dull, dirty, soiled, filthy **(dingy)**

- broadcast, pass on, send **(transmit)**

- desire for success, career goals, big plans **(ambition)**

- unexpected meeting, running into someone **(encounter)**

4 Read each sentence and ask students to decide if it is true or false. If the sentence is false, instruct students to explain why.

- An encounter is an appointment that you plan in advance. **(false; it is an unexpected meeting)**

- Dingy curtains make a room look prettier. **(false; dirty curtains make a room look worse)**

- Ambition can help people to achieve their goals. **(true)**

- Sneezing and coughing can transmit germs from one person to another. **(true)**

Answers for page 143: 1. B, 2. H, 3. A, 4. F

Name _____

ambition • dingy • transmit • encounter

Fill in the bubble next to the correct answer.

1. **Which word is a synonym for *encounter*?**
   Ⓐ farewell
   Ⓑ meeting
   Ⓒ beginning
   Ⓓ discussion

2. **Which word is a synonym for *transmit*?**
   Ⓕ receive
   Ⓖ halt
   Ⓗ send
   Ⓙ interrupt

3. **Which word is an antonym for *dingy*?**
   Ⓐ spotless
   Ⓑ patterned
   Ⓒ smooth
   Ⓓ shrunken

4. **Which word or phrase could be used instead of *ambition* in this sentence?**
   Writing and illustrating children's books is Katrina's ambition.
   Ⓕ goal
   Ⓖ current project
   Ⓗ difficult task
   Ⓙ job

Writing

Write about a job you'd like or another kind of goal you've set. Use **ambition** in your sentences.

_____

_____

bygone

adjective

anything that is past or has gone by

synonym: previous

Antique stores are full of things from **bygone** times.

Complete the graphic organizer for **bygone**.

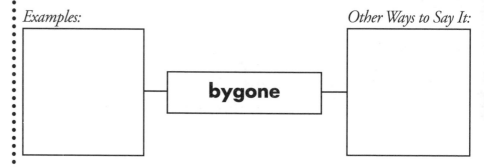

Examples:

bygone

Other Ways to Say It:

Give an example of something from a **bygone** time.

renovate

verb

to make like new

synonym: to restore

The school spent over one million dollars to **renovate** the old gym.

Which of the following can be **renovated**?

- an old house
- an Italian dinner
- a classic car
- a run-down neighborhood
- a Christmas tree

What structure in our town needs to be **renovated**?

bloated

adjective

swelled up

After eating six pieces of watermelon, my stomach was so **bloated** that I had to unbutton my pants.

Which words mean about the same thing as **bloated**?

- enlarged
- shrunken
- inflated
- hungry
- stretched

Have you ever felt like you were **bloated**? How did it feel?

velocity

noun

rate of speed or motion

A plane travels at a greater **velocity** than a car.

Which of the following can travel at a high **velocity**?

- a race car
- a horse and buggy
- a speedboat
- a bicycle built for two
- a supersonic jet

Name some things that travel at a low **velocity**.

bygone • renovate • bloated • velocity

Write on the board the four words studied this week. Read the words with the class and briefly review their meanings. Then conduct the oral activities below.

1 Tell students that you are going to give them a clue about one of the words for the week. They are to find the word that answers the clue.

- Someone may feel this way when his or her stomach is too full. **(bloated)**

- Homeowners sometimes do this to old houses. **(renovate them)**

- This word describes long-ago times. **(bygone)**

- A car's speedometer shows this. **(velocity)**

2 Read each sentence and ask students to supply the correct word to complete the sentence.

- Mr. White has bought an old factory. He plans to ____ it and make it his home. **(renovate)**

- On some freeways drivers may travel at a maximum ____ of 70 miles per hour. **(velocity)**

- The faces on the cartoon characters were so ____ they appeared about to burst. **(bloated)**

- In ____ times, my great-grandpa served in the army. **(bygone)**

3 Read each list of words and phrases. Ask students to supply the word that fits best with each.

- swollen, inflated, puffed up **(bloated)**

- remodel, restore, rebuild **(renovate)**

- previous, long ago, past **(bygone)**

- speed, quickness, rapidity **(velocity)**

4 Read each sentence and ask students to decide if it is true or false. If the sentence is false, instruct students to explain why.

- Having a bloated stomach feels uncomfortable. **(true)**

- Bygone times will happen in the future. **(false; they have already happened)**

- A bicycle travels at a greater velocity than a car. **(false; cars are speedier)**

- Workers who renovate homes include carpenters, plumbers, and painters. **(true)**

Answers for page 147: 1. C, 2. J, 3. B, 4. G

Name _____

Fill in the bubble next to the correct answer.

1. **Which word is an antonym for *bloated*?**
   - Ⓐ sickening
   - Ⓑ clogged
   - Ⓒ shrunken
   - Ⓓ swollen

2. **Which word is a synonym for *velocity*?**
   - Ⓕ length
   - Ⓖ depth
   - Ⓗ weight
   - Ⓙ speed

3. **How does someone *renovate* a home?**
   - Ⓐ by looking for a new home to buy
   - Ⓑ by rebuilding, repairing, and painting it
   - Ⓒ by offering the home for sale and selling it
   - Ⓓ by renting the home to someone else

4. **Which word or phrase could be used instead of *bygone* in this sentence?**
   In bygone days people had no phones, TVs, or computers.
   - Ⓕ recent
   - Ⓖ long-ago
   - Ⓗ happier
   - Ⓙ harder

Writing

Write about what you'd do if you could renovate one room in your home.
Use **renovate** in your sentences.

_____

_____

_____

Dictionary

Aa

abscond • *verb*

to run away suddenly and secretly

The bank robbers planned to abscond with thousands of dollars.

absorb • *verb*

1. to soak up liquid
2. to take in information

I read the instructions twice in order to absorb the information about how to absorb the paint I spilled on the rug.

absurd • *adjective*

without good sense

synonym: silly

It was absurd to try to eat the broth with a fork!

ache • *noun*

a dull, steady pain

After the doctor gave me a shot, I had an ache in my arm for a few days.

adapt • *verb*

to change in order to get along in a new situation

synonym: adjust

A chameleon can adapt to its surroundings by changing color to blend in with rocks and trees.

admonish • *verb*

to caution or warn

synonym: reprimand

Mrs. Wu had to admonish her students about running in the hallway.

advance • *verb*

to move forward or make progress

After I finished the books in Level One, I advanced to Level Two.

affluent • *adjective*

having a lot of money

synonym: wealthy

Marta loved to visit her affluent aunt because she had a swimming pool and a tennis court.

agriculture • *noun*

the science of growing crops and raising livestock

synonym: farming

My uncle studied agriculture in college and now grows organic tomatoes that he sells to restaurants.

ambition • *noun*

a strong desire to achieve a specific goal

Mark's ambition was to learn to surf.

amuse • *verb*

to make someone laugh or smile

The playful monkeys always amuse the visitors at the zoo.

atmosphere • *noun*

the mood or feeling of a place

The atmosphere during the test was quiet and serious.

Bb

baffled • *adjective*

confused or puzzled

synonym: perplexed

I was baffled by the complicated directions for assembling my new model car.

barricade

verb
to block off

noun
a barrier used to block passage

The fire department had to barricade the streets for the parade. They parked their firetrucks across the crosswalks to make a barricade.

barrier • *noun*

something that prevents things from going through

synonym: obstruction

The people made a barrier of sandbags to keep the river from flooding their town.

bedlam • *noun*

a scene of noise and confusion

synonym: chaos

There was bedlam on the decks of the Titanic when the ship began to sink.

belligerent • *adjective*

hostile; wanting to fight

The Peacemakers at our school use conflict resolution to help stop belligerent behavior.

betray • *verb*

to not be loyal or faithful to

Kin Yui didn't mean to betray Laura's secret when she told Ana. She thought Ana already knew about it.

bloated • *adjective*

swelled up

After eating six pieces of watermelon, my stomach was so bloated that I had to unbutton my pants.

boost • *noun*

something that lifts you up, either physically or emotionally

I couldn't reach the doorbell, so my brother gave me a boost.

brawl • *noun*

a loud fight

synonym: altercation

When the pitcher accidentally hit the batter with a fastball, a brawl broke out between the two teams.

bygone • *adjective*

anything that is past or has gone by

synonym: previous

Antique stores are full of things from bygone times.

Cc

candidate • *noun*

someone who is applying for a job or running in an election

Each candidate for school president gave a speech at the assembly.

cantankerous • *adjective*

hard to get along with

synonym: cranky

Because Jerry is so cantankerous, I already know he won't agree with me.

capable • *adjective*

having the skill to do something

synonym: competent

My little brother is capable of tying his shoes, but he asks for help anyway.

casual • *adjective*

1. happening by chance; not planned

2. informal; not fancy

When Jared's casual meeting with a friend led to a dinner invitation, he was glad his casual clothes were neat and clean.

classify • *verb*

to put into groups according to a system

Lilia will classify the insects in her collection by color.

collide • *verb*

to strike or bump together

If you don't watch where you're going, you can collide with someone.

command • *verb*

to order someone to do something

The trainer at the wild animal park commanded the wolf to bring him a stick.

compass • *noun*

a tool that can help you figure out in which direction you are facing

We knew that the camp was to the southwest, so we used our compass to help us find our way back to it.

compete • *verb*

to try to beat others in a race or contest

My cousin is training to compete in a bicycle race this summer.

complement • *noun*

something that makes something else complete

Cinderella's glass slippers were the perfect complement to her gown.

conceal • *verb*

to hide from view

I conceal my diary in a box under my bed so that no one will read it.

criticize • *verb*

to tell someone about what he or she has done wrong

Father criticized the young child's poor table manners.

curtail • *verb*

to cut short; reduce

synonym: shorten

Jeff's teacher suggested he curtail the time he spends playing video games if he wants to do better on his homework.

Dd

dapper • *adjective*

attractive in dress

synonym: fashionable

James was such a dapper dresser that he looked like a model.

dawdle • *verb*

to waste time; be slow

If you dawdle before breakfast, you'll miss your ride to school.

deceive • *verb*

to make someone believe something that is not true; to trick

synonym: lie

The wolf tried to deceive Little Red Riding Hood by dressing like her grandmother.

decline • *verb*

to turn down or refuse something

Mike had to decline the invitation to his friend's party because his family was going to be out of town.

defiant • *adjective*

bold in standing up against someone or something

The colonists were defiant when the king's soldiers ordered them to return home.

dejected • *adjective*

low in spirits

synonym: discouraged

Hiroshi felt dejected when he didn't break the record for the long jump.

destitute • *adjective*

having no money or other means of living

The fifth-graders raised money to help destitute people in their community.

determined • *adjective*

showing a firm decision to do something

No matter how tired he got, Harry was determined to finish the race.

detest • *verb*

to hate or strongly dislike

I don't like most vegetables, but what I really detest is cabbage.

devour • *verb*

to eat something very quickly or hungrily

Zoo visitors like to gather at feeding time to watch the cheetahs devour their steak.

dexterity • *noun*

skill in using the hands

After playing the piano for years, Mei-Ling has wonderful dexterity.

digits • *noun*

1. the numerals from zero through nine

2. fingers and toes

We have started adding numbers with three digits in math this week.

digress • *verb*

to get off the subject, especially when speaking or writing

The teacher took a moment to digress to tell a funny story before getting back to the lesson.

dilemma • *noun*

a situation that requires a difficult choice

synonym: predicament

Bonnie's dilemma was whether to attend her best friend's birthday party or play in the championship soccer game.

diligent • *adjective*

hardworking

Amy is a diligent student who always turns in her homework on time.

dingy • *adjective*

having a dirty or dull appearance

After years of hanging in the dusty windows, the white lace curtains looked dingy.

discussion • *noun*

a talk about things

synonym: conversation

Our teacher gathered us in a circle for a discussion about our upcoming field trip.

docile • *adjective*

easy to handle or train

Anita's docile dog won the prize for "best-behaved pet" at the show.

drenched • *adjective*

soaked or completely wet

We got drenched when we were caught out in the rain without an umbrella.

Ee

efficient • *adjective*

doing a job in a timely manner with the least amount of effort or materials

Pete was such an efficient busboy that he could stack and carry all the plates on the table at once.

elated • *adjective*

filled with joy

antonym: miserable

Jessica felt elated when she crossed the finish line first.

encounter • *noun*

an unexpected meeting

An encounter with a bear was the biggest surprise of our hike.

enthusiasm • *noun*

a strong feeling of excitement or interest

synonym: eagerness

Stella's enthusiasm for the ballet soon had the whole class eager to attend the performance.

establish • *verb*

to set up

The telephone company decided to first establish Internet service in large cities before setting it up in small towns.

exact • *adjective*

correct; having no mistakes

We need to know the exact measurements of the desk to be sure it will fit in my room.

Ff

fickle • *adjective*

always changing in interests or loyalty

We weren't surprised when Lisa switched teams at the last minute, because she is often fickle.

flounder

noun

a flatfish that lives in saltwater

verb

to struggle through something, either physically or mentally

After floundering through the deep, wet sand at the sea's edge, imagine my surprise at finding a flounder in the cuff of my pants.

foreign • *adjective*

1. from another country

2. different; strange

We served lots of foreign foods at the international celebration. The hamburgers looked foreign alongside all the other exotic foods.

frantic • *adjective*

very excited with worry or fear

Lihn was so frantic that she'd miss the bus for the field trip that she ran all the way to school.

frigid • *adjective*

extremely cold

There is no swimming in this mountain lake, as the water in it remains frigid even in the summer.

Gg

gallery • *noun*

a room or building where art is shown or sold

Ima was impressed by all the colorful paintings in the gallery.

germinate • *verb*

to begin to grow

synonym: sprout

The spring rains helped the wildflower seeds to germinate.

glamorous • *adjective*

attractive and exciting

synonym: enchanting

Heads turned as the glamorous movie star walked down the red carpet.

glitter • *verb*

to shine and sparkle

The crystal goblets are so clean that they glitter in the candlelight.

gloomy • *adjective*

1. dull and dark

2. sad

The gloomy weather on the day of the school picnic was mirrored by the gloomy expressions on the students' faces.

gossip • *verb*

to talk about other people's personal lives when they are not present

The neighbors gossiped about why the Wong family moved to New York, but no one really knew for sure.

gratitude • *noun*

a feeling of being grateful and thankful

When Dad gave me a new computer game, I showed my gratitude by giving him a big hug.

gregarious • *adjective*

fond of being with others

synonym: sociable

Because Heather is so gregarious, she always has friends around her.

Hh

habitat • *noun*

the home of a particular group of plants and animals

Although you might see a lion at a wild animal park, its natural habitat is the African savanna.

harass • *verb*

to bother repeatedly

My brother shoots rubber bands at me when he wants to harass me.

hazardous • *adjective*

dangerous

antonym: safe

A curvy road becomes even more hazardous during heavy rainstorms.

heirloom • *noun*

a valued object handed down from generation to generation

Alana's gold locket was a family heirloom that had belonged to her great-grandmother.

hemisphere • *noun*

one half of the Earth; there are four hemispheres: northern and southern; eastern and western

If you live in North America, you live in the northern and western hemispheres.

hermit • *noun*

a person who lives alone to be away from other people

synonym: recluse

The hermit saw other people only when he hiked into town to buy groceries.

hilarious • *adjective*

very funny

synonym: hysterical

The movie was so hilarious that we almost cried from laughing so hard.

humdrum • *adjective*

lacking variety or excitement

synonym: monotonous

The movie was so humdrum that I fell asleep.

Ii

ignore • *verb*

to pay no attention to something

If someone teases you, just ignore him or her and walk away.

indulge • *verb*

to allow yourself to enjoy something

Adrianne fought the urge to indulge her craving for the rich chocolate dessert.

ingenious • *adjective*

clever or skillful, especially at inventing or solving problems

The ingenious children made a skateboard using old roller skates and a piece of wood.

Jj

jumble • *noun*

a confused mess

The jumble of books in the box made it impossible to find what I was looking for.

justify • *verb*

to give a good reason or cause for something

Mark knew he could justify getting home from school late by explaining that the bus got a flat tire.

Kk

knickknack • *noun*

a small ornament or decorative object

synonym: trinket

The souvenir shop at the amusement park was full of knickknacks.

kowtow • *verb*

1. to show respect or unquestioning obedience
2. in traditional China, to bow from a kneeling position where the forehead touches the ground as a way to show respect

Although I am not required to get on the ground and kowtow to my parents, I am expected to kowtow to their wishes by never talking back to them.

Ll

lackadaisical • *adjective*

lacking interest, enthusiasm, or energy

Your piano playing won't improve if you have a lackadaisical attitude about practicing.

landscape

verb

to make the natural features of an outdoor area more attractive by adding trees or plants

noun

an area of land that you can view from one place

After we landscape the yard, the landscape outside the living room window will be more pleasant.

lecture

noun

a prepared talk about something

verb

to scold

The park ranger gave a lecture about wild animals. He told about having to lecture some campers about leaving food out for the bears.

legend • *noun*

a story that is handed down from the past that is often based on fact, but is not completely true

The legend of Johnny Appleseed is based on the life of a man named John Chapman.

lenient • *adjective*

not strict in enforcing rules and restrictions

synonym: permissive

Mrs. Johnson was so lenient about deadlines that most students turned in their projects late with no consequence.

lofty • *adjective*

1. very high
2. grand or noble

Roberta's lofty ambitions include designing lofty skyscrapers in New York City.

luminous • *adjective*

giving off light

The full moon was so luminous that Tim did not need a flashlight to see the path.

Mm

maneuver • *verb*

to move carefully and skillfully

Mika tried to maneuver his bike around the cones on the obstacle course.

marionette • *noun*

a puppet that is moved by pulling strings or wires attached to parts of its body

The puppeteer was so skilled in moving the marionette that the puppet almost seemed real.

massive • *adjective*

extraordinarily large, heavy, and solid

It took eight men to move the massive oak table into the moving van.

mischief • *noun*

playful behavior that often annoys or irritates others and may cause harm

The puppies' mischief stopped being funny when they chewed up Papi's new slippers.

moist • *adjective*

slightly wet or damp

I used a moist towel to wipe the pencil marks off my desk.

Nn

narrative • *noun*

a story or narration

Ms. Sanchez read the class a first-person narrative written by a soldier in the Civil War.

numerous • *adjective*

many; great in number

The curious student asked numerous questions during the science lesson.

Oo

obligation • *noun*

something that you must do

synonym: duty

After my birthday, one of my obligations was to write thank-you notes to the people who gave me gifts.

obvious • *adjective*

very easy to see or understand

It was obvious from the smile on her face that she was happy to see her grandmother.

outwit • *verb*

to be more clever than someone else

Edmond always won at chess because he could outwit any player he faced.

Pp

panic

noun

a sudden feeling of great fear that comes over a person or group of people

verb

to feel or be overcome by panic

I felt panic when I thought I'd lost my purse. "Don't panic!" said my friend. "It's right behind your chair."

participant • *noun*

someone who joins in an activity

The winner of the race will receive a medal, but all participants will receive a T-shirt.

patriot • *noun*

someone who loves and supports his or her country

During the American Revolution, many patriots fought against the British for the independence of the colonies.

peer • *noun*

a person of the same age or ability level

Even though Daisy is Roberto's peer, she is three inches taller than he is.

penetrate • *verb*

to go into or pass through something

The attackers could not penetrate the stone walls of the castle.

perennial

adjective

lasting for a long time; never ending

noun

a plant that blooms or grows for many years without needing to be replanted

If you have a perennial dislike for buying new plants every year, plant some perennials in your garden.

permanent • *adjective*

lasting for a very long time or forever

Baby teeth fall out, but permanent teeth do not.

perplexed • *adjective*

confused; uncertain

I was perplexed because the directions to the museum did not make sense to me.

plunge • *verb*

1. to dive into water
2. to fall sharply

Standing at the edge of the boat, my heart plunged as I watched my necklace plunge into the sea.

precious • *adjective*

1. rare and valuable
2. special or dear

My most precious possession is this ring with four precious gems in the setting.

predicament • *noun*

a difficult, dangerous, or unpleasant situation

The sailors were in a predicament when the mainsail ripped.

purchase • *verb*

to buy something

Our family tries to purchase things when they're on sale.

Rr

random • *adjective*

not following any pattern or order

The teacher put everyone's name in a jar and drew the teams in random order.

recommend • *verb*

to praise the value of something; suggest as worthwhile

synonym: endorse

I recommend you try the milkshakes at the local diner; they're delicious!

remedy

noun

a medicine or treatment used for healing

verb

to return something to its proper condition

Adam's mother gave him mint tea as a remedy for his upset stomach. She hoped it would remedy his stomachache quickly.

renovate • *verb*

to make like new

synonym: to restore

The school spent over one million dollars to renovate the old gym.

replenish • *verb*

to refill

After the long race, the runners had to replenish the water in their bodies.

resource • *noun*

a person or thing that is a source of help or support

The library is a great resource for learning about American history.

rickety • *adjective*

likely to fall over or fall apart due to weakness

The rickety old fence blew over with the first strong winter wind.

Ss

scavenger • *noun*

an animal that eats already dead and decaying animals

The deer's carcass was soon picked clean by vultures and other scavengers.

shrub • *noun*

a plant that has several woody stems instead of a trunk

synonym: bush

The yard looked beautiful now that several of the shrubs were blooming.

sluggish • *adjective*

moving slowly; lacking energy

After eating a big lunch and resting in the hammock, I felt so sluggish that I could barely move.

solo • *noun*

a performance by one performer

You could tell that Anoki had been practicing, because he performed his solo perfectly.

spontaneous • *adjective*

happening without planning

I wasn't expecting the joke to be funny, but I let out a spontaneous laugh.

stagnant • *adjective*

not moving or flowing

synonym: still

When a puddle of water is stagnant, harmful bacteria can grow in it.

symphony • *noun*

a long piece of music played by an orchestra

The famous composer Mozart wrote a symphony that was nicknamed "Jupiter."

Tt

tedious • *adjective*

boring; tiresome

Three hours of weeding a garden can be tedious.

temporary • *adjective*

something that lasts only for a short time

The power outage was temporary; our electricity was back on by morning.

thaw • *verb*

to melt after being frozen

The frozen turkey must thaw in the refrigerator for three days before we can cook it.

transmit • *verb*

1. to pass on from one person or place to another
2. to send out signals by radio or television

When the flu season begins, people try not to transmit their germs. Some radio stations even transmit information on how to stay healthy.

treacherous • *adjective*

dangerous; hazardous

Skydiving and mountain climbing can be treacherous sports.

trivial • *adjective*

of little or no importance

My tiny scratch seemed trivial next to Drew's broken arm.

Uu

unique • *adjective*

someone or something that is the only one of its kind

A fish that could survive on dry land would be unique.

unkempt • *adjective*

not groomed; not neat or tidy

After a week of camping in the wilderness, everybody looked quite unkempt.

unruly • *adjective*

hard to control; wild

The unruly crowd went wild when the rock stars appeared.

Vv

vanquish • *verb*

to defeat; overcome

synonym: conquer

Zack had to vanquish his fear of the dark before going camping with his friends.

velocity • *noun*

rate of speed or motion

A plane travels at a greater velocity than a car.

ventriloquist • *noun*

an entertainer who speaks without moving his or her lips

The ventriloquist made it look like his wooden dummy was telling the jokes.

Ww

weary • *adjective*

tired or exhausted

Mom was weary after driving for almost three days to get to Grandma's house.

Examples:

Other Ways to Say It:

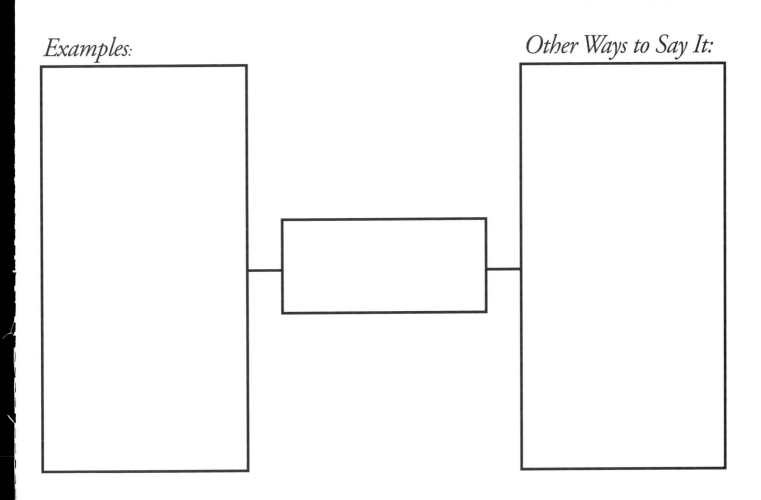

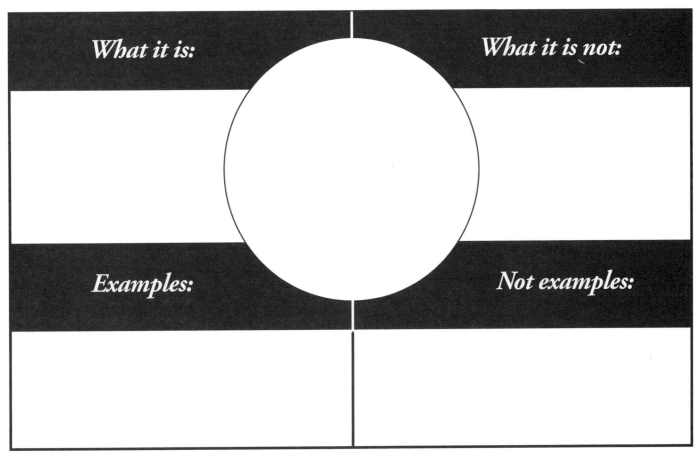

What it is:

What it is not:

Examples:

Not examples:

Index